COUNTRY MUSIC READER 2007

COUNTRY MUSIC READER 2007

Foreword by Rosanne Cash • Edited by Randy Rudder

Music City Book Publishing

Copyright © 2006 by Randy Rudder

Publisher's Cataloging-In-Publication Data
(Prepared by The Donohue Group, Inc.)

Country music reader 2007 / foreword by Rosanne Cash ; edited by Randy Rudder.

p. ; cm.

ISBN-13: 978-0-9769745-1-2
ISBN-10: 0-9769745-1-7

1. Country music—History and criticism. 2. Bluegrass music—History and criticism. 3. Country musicians—United States. 4. Bluegrass musicians—United States. I. Rudder, Randy. II. Cash, Rosanne. III. Cooper, Peter M., 1970- IV. DeMain, Bill. V. Tyrangiel, Josh. VI. Goldsmith, Thomas, 1952- VII. Cronin, Peter. VIII. Doerschuk, Bob. IX. Proctor, Danny. X. Friskics-Warren, Bill. XI. Roland, Tom. XII. Hood, John. XIII. Nash, Alanna. XIV. Kelly, Rick. XV. Stuart, Chris. XVI. McCall, Michael. XVII. Weisberger, Jon. XVIII. Scarlett, David. XIX. Flippo, Chet, 1943- XX. Himes, Geoffrey.

ML3524 .M87 2006
781.642

Music City Book Publishing
2496 Port Kembla Dr.
Mt Juliet, TN 37122

Cover and book design: KerseyGraphics www.kerseygraphics.com

DEDICATION

In memory of Dr. Charles Wolfe (1943—2006), MTSU professor and author: the quintessential music scholar, who helped expose country music to the world, who readily shared with others, and who left a wonderful legacy both to his biological family, and to the family of academics, authors, and journalists he left behind.

"*A good name is to be desired above riches.*" Proverbs 22:1

Contents

Foreword .... *viii*

Acknowledgments .... *xv*

"Rosanne Cash Shares Her Pain" *1*
   By Peter Cooper
   From *The Tennessean*

**"Emmylou Harris & Mark Knopfler:
The Road Runs from Nashville to Notting Hill"** *9*
   By Bill DeMain
   From *Performing Songwriter*

"The Dixie Chicks: In the Line of Fire" *23*
   By Josh Tyrangiel
   From *Time*

**"It Was the Singing: A Conversation with
Mac Wiseman"** *33*
   By Thomas Goldsmith
   From *Bluegrass Unlimited*

"Carrie Underwood's Wild Ride" *43*
   By Peter Cronin
   From *CMA Close Up*

"Matraca Berg: Pensive Behind the Pen" *49*
   By Robert L. Doerschuk
   From *American Songwriter*

"George Jones" 57
    By Danny Proctor
    From *Music City News*

"To Beat the Devil: Intimations of Immortality"
(Kris Kristofferson) 65
    By Bill Friskics-Warren
    From *No Depression*

"Buck Owens: 1929-2006" 87
    By Tom Roland
    From *Country Weekly*

"Climbing to the Top of the Duo Heap:
An Interview With Troy Gentry 93
    By John Hood
    From *Music City News*

"Songs of Faith" 99
    By Alanna Nash
    From *Country Weekly*

"Bobby Bare: The Return of the Quiet Outlaw" ... 109
    By Rick Kelly
    From *CMA Close Up*

"Del McCoury: Leading Man" 115
    By Chris Stuart
    From *Bluegrass Unlimited*

**"Faith Hill Never Stopped
Being a Mississippi Girl"** *129*
    By Michael McCall
    From *CMA Close Up*

**"Brad Paisley Moves up from
Corn Dogs to Catered Meals"** *135*
    By Peter Cooper
    From *The Tennessean*

"Earl Scruggs: The Godfather of Bluegrass" *141*
    By Jon Weisberger
    From *The Nashville Scene*

"Why George Is Still On Top" (George Strait) *149*
    By David Scarlett
    From *Country Weekly*

"Just What the Hell Is Country Music, Anyway?" .. *153*
    By Chet Flippo
    ("Nashville Skyline" Column)
    From CMT.com

"Alecia Nugent" *157*
    By Geoffrey Himes
    From *Bluegrass Unlimited*

Contents

"Women Make Inroads into Realm of Record Production" *169*
    By Peter Cooper
    From *The Tennessean*

Contributors *175*

Permissions *178*

FOREWORD

In the summer of 1994, I spent a couple of weeks alone in Paris, working on my first book of short stories, *Bodies of Water*. One late afternoon, I put aside my heavily scribbled yellow legal pads, left them on the tiny desk in my hotel and went for a walk. I strolled down a narrow street in the Latin Quarter and suddenly I heard the notes of an acoustic guitar, and the voice of my old friend Guy Clark, wafting out of the open doorway of a little record shop. I stopped in mid-stride to listen to the song. I was happily disoriented. Guy Clark? Paris?

I edged slowly into the store and surveyed rack upon rack of vinyl records, all of them by American country, folk and roots musicians. I was ecstatic. I started flipping through the records, recognizing friends, heroes, legends, journeymen and women, songwriters, stars, and pickers. I suddenly came upon my own records. At that very moment, the owner of the shop came up to me and said with authority, as he pointed to one of my records, "Non, non, non. This one is not good." He flipped past a couple of albums and pulled out *King's Record Shop*, a landmark record for me from 1988. He handed it to me. "This one. This is a great record." I looked at him and smiled. He still didn't make the connection. I thought for a second, and then said quietly, "It's me."

"Oui, oui," he said impatiently, not understanding. I self-consciously raised the album up next to my face. "C'est moi. It's me."

"Oh, my God!" He gasped.

We laughed.

Foreword

I remembered that experience as I read the essays, articles, and interviews in this wonderful compilation. I came to these stories as a fan, I happily thumbed through the stories, and I made connections to my own work and my own life in these pieces written about friends, mentors, heroes, enigmas, and colleagues. They were also written by friends, mentors, heroes, enigmas and colleagues, so the content mirrors the context, and there is a consensus of respect and a shared love and passion for this particular kind of music among both writer and subject.

There are some writers here who have been doing this so long and have achieved a level of such mastery that they have attained a kind of fabled status in the pantheon of music journalists: they are nearly as sought out as the artists they write about. Chet Flippo was the very first writer to interview me when my debut record for Columbia was about to be released in 1980. I spoke to him in my father's apartment at 40 Central Park South in New York City in late 1979. I was 24 years old, pregnant, and had purple hair. I was very nervous, and he was very gracious, and that initial interview set the tone for the following 28 years of interviews and my relationships with music journalists in general. I understood it was a forum for mutual respect, grace, connection and a real understanding of the pressures and joy of the other's profession.

There are other masters here besides Chet, and some friends as well: Alanna Nash, Jon Weisberger, Michael McCall, Bill Friskics-Warren and Peter Cooper; there are also up-and-comers, writers who are poets at heart, salarymen, scientists and analysts, and those whose voices are as unique as any singer.

From Charlie Lamb's *Country Music Reporter* in the 1950's, to *Rolling Stone* and *No Depression* today, the field of country music journalism has evolved along with the music

Foreword

itself. These interviews, features, and essays are the current endpoint of that evolution. They span the spectrum from poetry to commercial inspection, and all are worthy of deliberation.

There is a certain familiarity and familial quality between country music journalists and artists, more so than in other musical genres. That may change as clear definitions about what is 'country,' and what is not, transform over time, and as the marketplace becomes more and more niche-defined and fragmented. But, for this moment, reading through these essays provoke—at least in me—a blessed familiarity, comforting and inspiring, just as I felt thumbing through the album racks in a tiny shop in Paris, with the voice of a friend singing around me, on a warm afternoon with nothing else to do.

Rosanne Cash
August, 2006

ACKNOWLEDGMENTS

If you, by chance, looked for the second edition of the *Music City Reader* and couldn't find it, this is it. Your favorite country music anthology has a new look, a new feel, a new name, a new price, and of course, an entirely new collection of interviews, articles, and essays about your favorite country and bluegrass singers and songwriters. When I tried to sell the book last year in places like Austin, Memphis, Detroit, and New Orleans, there was a little confusion as to exactly which *Music City* we were writing about, since all of those cities have their musical traditions as well. I trust with the new *Country Music Reader* title, the book's contents will be perfectly clear.

As with the previous edition, the new *Country Music Reader* couldn't have been assembled without the assistance of people like publishers Mark Renz, Emma Wisdom, and Maryglenn McCombs. Thank you for your guidance and consulting.

Thanks to all the folks at the International Country Music Conference like Ronnie Pugh, James Akenson, Jay Orr, Wayne Daniel, and Ted Olson.

Thanks to Brenda Colladay, Beverly Keel, Don Cusic, and Cathie Pelletier for being willing to review the book.

Thanks to Cathy Gurley, my publicist, for your enthusiasm and direction on this project.

Thanks to designer Bill Kersey for a great cover and photographer Jon LeMay for a great photo.

Thanks to Charlie Lamb, the first country music journalist in Nashville.

Thanks to my wife Clare Rudder for being a sounding

Acknowledgments

board and for sacrificing a lot of lonely nights.

Thanks to David Covington for your proofreading expertise.

Thanks to all the contributors to this edition for your excellent work. You are all true artists in your own right.

ROSANNE CASH SHARES HER PAIN

Black Cadillac isn't so much the story of a famous family as it is of a grieving daughter

By Peter Cooper
From *The Tennessean*

GLENSIDE, PA. — The sign on the Keswick Theatre marquee said "Kristofferson & Cash," a billing that caused passers-by to check the date and make sure it was April 2, 2006, and not the day or decade before.

Hours before playing the co-billed show with Country Music Hall of Famer Kris Kristofferson, Rosanne Cash pondered Kristofferson's willingness to integrate politics and music.

"Kris has nothing to lose, and, truthfully, neither do I," said the 50-year-old, whose current album, *Black Cadillac*, is not distinguished by its themes of ancestry, of loss, of memory and transcendence. It is distinguished by the emotional clarity she brings to those themes and by the universality she manages even as she writes about the aftermath of the deaths of her mother, Vivian Liberto Distin, her stepmother, June Carter Cash, and her father, the iconic Johnny Cash.

"Who do I need to please? Nobody," she continued.

"Who do I need to rebel against or report to? Nobody, anymore. That's the thing about losing your parents. No one to rebel against, nobody to report to."

Cash speaks such words with a combination of frailty, resignation and matter-of-factness. She spent much of her early artistic life trying to make her way around her father's shadow, only to find that shadows can serve as blankets.

"I miss the sounds of Tennessee and the smell of heavy rain," she writes in "House on the Lake," a song set at John and June's Hendersonville estate, recently sold to pop star Barry Gibb. "I hear his voice, I follow down the velvet undertow / Back to the place where I was born / Back to my Southern home."

Cash is a New Yorker now, and has been for a decade and a half. She's happy there, living in the Chelsea area and married to producer / guitar virtuoso John Leventhal.

She was born in Memphis, where her parents' marriage began to dissolve and where her father's career began to rise. Most of her Tennessee memories, though, are of Middle Tennessee, a place that holds complicated memories of the house on the lake, the early phases of her recording career, a difficult but creatively fulfilling marriage to singer-songwriter luminary Rodney Crowell and an exit from a country music mainstream through which she'd scored hits in the '80s including "Seven Year Ache," "The Way We Make a Broken Heart," "Tennessee Flat-Top Box," "Blue Moon With Heartache," and "Runaway Train."

Raised in Los Angeles, Cash felt herself something of an outsider to Nashville's industry-peculiar modus operandi.

"I didn't realize there was this game to play, a line to toe and you were on the road this many days a year and you treated your fans like this and you dress like this and you showed up at this and at that," she said. "I just didn't get it. I wasn't rebelling against it, I just didn't even know it was there."

Following her string of hits and facing the end of her marriage to Crowell, Cash released the sparse, folksy *Interiors* album in 1990. The record company, Columbia's Nashville division, balked at the album's less-than-commercial nature. Company brass said country radio wouldn't play it, Cash said *Interiors* was the direction she was heading, and ultimately she was told, "Thanks, we'll miss you."

In Nashville, the turn of that decade saw numerous changes. The rootsy, lyric-heavy country movement that Steve Earle referred to as Music City's "credibility scare of the 1980s" was over, and artists such as Cash, Crowell, Earle, Emmylou Harris, Lyle Lovett and Nanci Griffith were no longer considered part of country's hip mainstream. Cash and Crowell had been that movement's power couple—the Tim and Faith of the pre-Americana set—and now that scene and marriage were dissipating.

"To end a 12-year career with a handshake and a 20-minute conversation was sad," she said. "It was difficult for me, and I was also in the process of getting a divorce and moving to New York. It was a huge time of change for me.

"Then I started reading these things about how I'd turned my back on Nashville and I was the one that was bitter. It was hurtful, because it went with a lot of ugly rumors that I was having affairs, that I was a lesbian, that I was . . . there was so much I read that I couldn't believe. But, you know what, it was good. Clearing that house. Open the widows."

Those windows stayed wide open for the next few years. Cash fell in love, married Leventhal and released two albums that were critically hailed but commercially tepid. She turned to short fiction, writing a book of short stories. (Since then, she has written a children's book and compiled a book of prose efforts by celebrated songwriters.)

"These things opened up a whole new world for me," she said. "Commercial failure is one of the best things that can happen to you after you've been successful. Really, it is."

There is, of course, family history to back her notion about the benefits of failure. Some of Johnny Cash's most remarkable recordings came after he had been deemed commercially expendable by Music Row decision makers. The father hooked up with California-based producer Rick Rubin in the 1990s and made his thrilling series of *American Recordings*. The daughter anchored in New York and honed her skills in prose and in song-poems.

"The future's like a ringing bell," she wrote in "Dreams Are Not My Home" from *Black Cadillac*. "The road to good intentions wanders all the way through hell."

Last year, Sony Legacy reissued several of Rosanne Cash's Nashville-based albums. Cash examined 25 years of her back catalog for the first time in recent memory, listening to songs like most people pull out books of old family photographs or re-read letters that had been long ago stuffed in drawers. The recordings were marks on a timeline. *Interiors* seemed like a point of embarkation, not a dead end. And Cash could live well with the whole thing.

"I still think of myself as a new artist in some ways, and I know that sounds strange," she said.

Tributes abounded in the wake of the deaths of Johnny and June Carter Cash. Some of these existed because there is money to be made from rosy memories, others for less crass reasons, but the fact was that Americans were more likely to wear Cash T-shirts, watch Cash on television or look at Cash billboards after Sept. 12, 2003, than before. Cash's children walked their own line, between appreciating the well-wishes and craving privacy.

"In normal circumstances, you would be allowed the

time to process your grief, and then to get some distance so you can get back to your own life," Cash said. "Me and my sisters and my brother, we've never gotten any distance."

Strangers send songs they've written about Johnny Cash, or they approach Rosanne in bookstores or cafes with stories about her father and stepmother.

"It's sweet, and I respect that and it's an honor," she said. "But it can get burdensome. I have to protect my own emotions, because I can't let myself be dragged to that place a dozen times a day. It's just too painful."

Cash said this as she was preparing to stand before a mentor and hero (Kristofferson) and an audience of strangers and sing about her father's war years, the now-sold house in Hendersonville and her own grief.

As a veteran writer, she has found a way to make these things relatable to listeners who cannot know what it is to have family and fame so interwoven, but as a person who wants to protect private emotions, the process would seem like leaving the keys in the ignition and the doors unlocked and hoping the car doesn't get stolen.

"Actually, the process helped bring a sense of order to these chaotic, overwhelming feelings," she said. "To bring your discipline as a writer and a sense of poetry, it starts to make sense and to transcend just being your own thing."

She recorded the songs, some with Leventhal and some with California producer Bill Bottrell, and determined their running order. Then, with the project ostensibly completed, on Cash's 50th birthday, her mother died of lung cancer. Six weeks later, she wrote "Like Fugitives," and cried through the song's recording. It is the album's angriest song, with lyrics that seem to address her mother's worries about the Cash biopic *Walk the Line* ("She was so dreading the film," Rosanne said), in which Liberto Distin was depicted as less than supportive of Johnny Cash's music.

"The only truth believed in is the one up on the screen / So we live our lives like fugitives when we were born to live like queens," Cash sings.

While her father and stepmother were well-loved public figures, Cash's mother eschewed fame.

"She was incredibly private," Cash said. "She was first and foremost a mother. She didn't want a public life. But she was active in her church, she was president of her garden club, and the house she made was incredibly open and welcoming.

"You know, she developed relationships with disc jockeys because she'd call them up to tell them to play my records and she'd become friends with them."

Leventhal was playing guitar in a Keswick Theatre stairwell, warming up for the show, while Cash talked about her mother. The world didn't know Vivian enough to grieve for her, which makes Cash's feelings no less intense. We are all famous to our friends, and many of us are icons to our children.

"Nobody is ever going to lose Johnny Cash," she said that afternoon. "So grief at losing my father is the same grief everyone experiences with the loss of a parent."

When she took the stage and sang songs from *Black Cadillac*, the connection with the audience was not due to any sense of diary-reading or Cash mythologizing. It was due to the collective natures of loss, grief and confusion, and to the way a skillful writer and singer can evoke honest emotion.

Rosanne Cash gets mail sometimes from people who hear doubt in her lyrics, who fear she is fractured, who think she is hungry for salvation and who want to save her soul.

Then, on a glorious spring night in a Philadelphia suburb, she appears with her husband, stands up to a microphone, strums a guitar and sings, "God is in the roses, and the thorns."

Peter Cooper

Emmylou Harris & Mark Knopfler:
The Road Runs from Nashville to Notting Hill

By Bill DeMain
From *Performing Songwriter*

Summer 1975. The country music charts are under siege. From the glitz of Glen Campbell's "Rhinestone Cowboy" to the faux-bumpkin bounce of John Denver's "Thank God I'm a Country Boy," the down-home essence of the music was being nudged out by radio-friendly MOR pop. The cavalry comes in the form of a winsome former folkie named Emmylou Harris, who sails into the charts with "If I Could Only Win Your Love." An acolyte of Gram Parsons, Harris fuses a hard-core attitude with a west coast poetic spin to make country hip again.

Four years later, the pop charts are experiencing a similar crisis that can be summed up in two words: disco sucks. While punk is galvanizing the underground, the mainstream needs rescue from the swollen excess of songs like "Bad Girls" and "Do Ya Think I'm Sexy?" It comes from England with "Sultans of Swing," a five-minute tour de force of Dylan-esque lyrics and blistering Stratocaster licks by Mark Knopfler and his band Dire Straits. There is something reassuring in hearing Knopfler's husky voice say, "You feel all right when you hear the music ring."

Thirty years after their debuts, these two venerated musicians have joined forces for *All The Roadrunning*, an album of duets that captures the best of their distinct personalities.

"I suppose our paths were bound to cross," says Harris. "We talked about the fact that we probably listened to a lot of the same music, and our radar was attuned to the music that was the real washed-in-the-blood stuff. I think we were going against the current, both of us. Our collaboration makes sense. But I never in a million years would've conceived of this record that is here now. I said to somebody, 'I feel like this is my gift for thirty years of faithful service in the music business.'"

We interviewed Harris from her home in Nashville and Knopfler via phone from England. Here are their thoughts on songcraft, the art of collaborating, and the emotional distance of British male singers.

Emmylou Harris

You've sung with a lot of singers who have very idiosyncratic styles, from Johnny Cash to Willie Nelson. What was the challenge of singing with Mark?

His voice is in a nice low register, which puts me in a nice medium part of my voice, where I've been doing more and more singing, anyway. So I didn't have to worry about going up and getting impossibly high notes. It was very natural singing with him. We didn't have to labor over it. Also, we had the conversation going. Specifically in songs like "This Is Us" or in "Love And Happiness," where it's the mother speaking and it's the father speaking. So we're not necessarily trying to be a romantic duo, although we can play those roles. I think there's a wonderful world of experience that we bring to this album that is showcased, especially in Mark's writing. It was a very natural situation in which everything seemed to click.

Having worked with Mark, and also Elvis Costello recently, and knowing that you were married to an English musician, I'm curious about your thoughts on the subject of British male singer-songwriters and emotionality.

That's an interesting question. I think that they have absorbed the best of American music, without the filter or something. Country music and roots music seems like it's appreciated overseas, especially in England, more so than over here. I don't know whether it's because we haven't had access to it on radio over here, until recently. Perhaps because it's harder to get the records over there, it becomes like searching for treasure.

Speaking of my ex-husband Paul Kennerly, he's a great friend of Mark's. It was really through my friendship with Paul — we're still friends — that I socialized with Mark. Paul got introduced to country music through a Waylon Jennings album called *Dreaming My Dreams*, and decided he wanted to write country music. But he thought, "Well, I don't have any experience." So he read everything that he could on the Civil War and then he wrote "White Mansions," which is a brilliant exercise in songwriting. I'm digressing a little bit, but of course I know Paul's experience the most. He knows how to separate the chaff from the wheat, the stuff that he calls music that's washed in the blood. Artists like Elvis Costello and Mark have this radar that puts them in touch with the stuff that really resonates, and then they make it their own. They put it through their own cultural experience.

Bill DeMain

What I find interesting too is that there's this cliche of the British male as being emotionally reserved and yet so many of them who are musicians seem to find this great outlet in their songwriting.

    I read something once, in a critique of a poet that was talking about her poetry and describing the way she was able to be successful. It said that restraint intensifies emotion. I always thought that was a good way to describe a lot of things. I think that there's nothing wrong with restraint. Sometimes a little restraint is required in order to really intensify what you're trying to say. If everybody could just sing their journals - I think there are actually a lot of artists who tend to do that. But that doesn't necessarily make a really good song. You might have a lot of feeling, but you need to have structure. It's extremely important in art, any kind of art. Even Picasso, who could've drawn anything. Because he was so advanced in his talents at an early age, he was able to break outside the lines. You have to have that center of knowing how to work within the parameters.
    I don't know whether English people are more restrained. I think that they tend to be raised right and have good manners. What's restrained about the Rolling Stones? They learned all the Muddy Waters stuff. They learned how to play the blues, and then they were able to go off and become the Rolling Stones.

Restraint might not be the exact word, but there's a characteristic that's common in my favorite vocalists, in that they don't have to go overboard with vocalizing to get an emotion across. You certainly have that.

    I think learning to sing in the arena of country music was behind that. It was Gram Parsons who got me into country music, and harmonizing with him, which required even more restraint. Basically, you're just learning to trust the melody and the lyric. We're all just servants to the music. It's not about putting the spotlight on yourself; it's about putting the spotlight on the song. That's the only guide.

And also, to be brutally honest, I don't have the kind of chops where I can do those kinds of things that I hear other singers do. Fortunately, I don't usually do the kinds of songs that require that. I don't know if any song requires it. Sometimes I think the only person that should ever be allowed to do it is Aretha Franklin (laughs). After that, it's like why should anyone else even attempt it? She's so brilliant. It's like going to another stratosphere with her, but somehow you never feel that she's showing off.

The theme of this issue is collaboration. The first and perhaps most significant example of that for you was with Gram Parsons. What did you learn about collaboration from that experience?

It's just like Ginger Rogers and Fred Astaire. I had to learn to follow. Yet the beauty of a real duet, even though one person is doing the harmony and one person is doing the melody, [is that] one person sort of sets the pace. That's not the right word. But ultimately, it becomes totally equal. You're in a certain kind of sync, because once again, you're following the song. It's still the song. Once again, Gram taught me that if you're going to find the true emotional reading of the song, it's going to basically come from plugging yourself into the song.

In the case of duets, there's that synchronicity of following each other. Then there's the sound of the third voice that is created by the two voices, because every voice is totally unique. When you add those two unique voices, you're going to come up with another voice. Not that you're *thinking* about all that while you're doing it. It's just the act. I suppose it's something where you lose yourself in the process. It's an odd thing. You're extremely present, but you're also outside of it, in a strange sort of way.

If he had lived, what kind of music do you think Gram would be doing today?

Gram was always ahead of his time. I think he would definitely be doing good music. He loved good music, but wasn't prissy about it. He wasn't a purist. But he understood real country music enough to have the ability to do that. Once again, getting back to being able to know the rules so you can break the rules. When he wrote "Sin City" with Chris Hillman, they were using a very traditional country-bluegrass form, with those chord structures and everything, the melody even. And yet, the lyrics were apocalyptic. They were reinventing themselves poetically, which is what every generation has to do. It's just not enough to go back and recreate music that was made in the 1950s.

How do you go about finding songs today?

I'm in this state right now where I'm saying, "Okay, I'm going to write my material." But I've been pretty busy, and I haven't written anything in a while. So I found myself going back to old favorites that I always meant to record, and just as an exercise, going into the studio and doing some things. I haven't found any new songs. I make tapes of songs that I always thought that one day I'd like to record. Most of the songs have been recorded before. Like a favorite Merle Haggard song. I think they just find their way to me.

Do you have a big record collection?

Yeah. And now I have people giving me iPods that they've programmed. Elvis Costello gave me one. I call it the Elvis iPod (laughs).

What's on it?

It's everything from beautiful classical music to wonderful old blues, jazz and world music. Just incredible stuff. Every once in a while, you'll hear something and you'll have to wake yourself out of sleep and turn the light on to see what you're hearing. So friends turn you on to songs. I think you just have to listen. Satellite radio has been great. I listen to either the folk channel or the old country channel or the outlaw channel. Sometimes on XM, I listen to the '40s, '50s and '60s channel. It's hard to keep up. I'm in the music business, and I get overwhelmed. I go to a record store, and I don't even know where to begin. I just trust that they're going to find their way to me. I don't obsess over it.

Is it true that you wrote a letter to Pete Seeger when you were a kid?

I did. I wasn't a kid. I was a full-blown teenager, about sixteen. I wanted to be a folk singer, but I didn't feel that I had the right because I'd never suffered (laughs). It was rather charming and naive. Pete wrote back saying, "I wouldn't worry about that" (laughs). He didn't say that you'll suffer soon enough, but basically he was saying that life will come at you like a freight train, so don't worry about it. But what a lovely man to take the time to write to a little girl who was stuck in suburbia, in Woodbridge, Virginia. I spent five hours every night sitting in my room listening to Dick Serry doing his folk show from American University while I was doing my homework. I really had no social life. I had a wonderful family. You know, darn it (laughs). I couldn't blame them for anything. I had wonderful, loving parents, and I never went hungry. So it was like, "How could I have any credibility?" But boy, was Pete right.

You are one of the busiest artists in any genre, just in terms of guest appearances, touring, TV tapings. What drives you?

I don't know if I'm driven so much as I'm so fortunate with the opportunities that come my way. How could you *not* record and tour with Elvis Costello? Then I did the album with Neil Young, and he says that we're going to record and film it with Jonathan Demme at the Ryman. "Nah, I don't think I'll do that" (laughs). I mean, here are artists who have inspired me. I love music. I really do love music. And I love collaboration because the pressure's not on you. So instead of taking a vacation sailing around the world, I got to work with Elvis and Neil last year. Then of course, the album with Mark. It's like, somebody up there must really like me. At some point, I'm going to have to get back to scratching my head, and say, "Okay, what am I going to do now?" I'll get around to that, but right now, there's really no pressure. I mean, there's always a little pressure. It's part of my personality. I want to be working in some way. It's like working out at the gym. It's not like you're going to run a marathon, but you want to make sure that your body is in good shape when the time comes.

Emmylou's Essential Listening:
Bruce Springsteen: *Nebraska*. It inspired me to make

some big changes, to get off the touring wheel that I was on, and really put my mind to finishing certain little ideas that I had. And that's what happened with *The Ballad of Sally Rose*. The album was a commercial disaster, but I'll never regret doing it. It proved that I could get an idea and follow it through, with the help of Paul Kennerly. That is the most specific example of an album affecting me.

As far as what affects my songwriting, that's probably more like an osmosis thing of just years of listening to great songwriters. Roseanne Cash is an extraordinary writer. She almost stopped me from writing. Every time she would come up with a song, I would go, "That's my life and I didn't even know it."

Bob Dylan created a whole new world. Everybody who's writing today, in my generation, was probably affected by Bob Dylan. Because everything became possible. Language took on a whole new life with Bob Dylan.

I remember the first time I heard The Band. There was a lot of great stuff in the '60s, but boy, when you first heard "The Weight." I remember I was walking down St. Mark's Place in the Village on a beautiful spring day, and it was being played in some store. It just stopped me in my tracks. It was like having a religious experience.

I still believe in classic song structures and writers like Boudleaux Bryant, where the rhyme had to be a classic rhyme. You couldn't cheat, where a rhyme kind of sounded right. Boy, that's hard to do. When you can write a song like that, you can really sit back and light up a cigarette and say, "Yeah, I did it."

Mark Knopfler

What is it about Emmylou's voice that attracts you the most?

Emmy has a real love of folk music, and you could hear that in her voice from the beginning. Folk music is a place which we both come from. When she was young, there was this tremendous purity, but I think Emmy brings an awful lot more to a song now. I really find that when I hear her taking on a song, I see the characters immediately. She's serious about what she does.

She and I were talking about British singer-songwriters and their fascination with American music. Of course the irony is that much of that music has its root in folk songs from the UK. Do you think that there's a kind of genetic longing at work there?

Good question. I wish I could answer that. People wonder how you can invent something that sounds so old, but I think you just have to love it in the first place. I think that's true of music generally. I don't necessarily think it's Celtic music, per se, or anything like that. Although I certainly do feel, with having been born in Scotland and living in the north of England, that I'm at home with Celtic music. It's as natural as anything to me. I felt the same thing about boogie woogie too, that it was as natural and cosmic. It's all folk music, really, in the end. It almost doesn't matter what it is. The more time you spend in connection with it, you realize that it's all just music. It all relates in some way or another. There's an awful lot to be said for listening to the box sets of great artists. I'm not saying that you should listen exclusively to old music. But being reasonably familiar with it gives you some depth in your songwriting. I'm fortunate that I've spent time delving around in the roots of the music, both black and white. That probably informs a little of what I do.

Along with folk music, it's always been clear that literature has been a major influence on your songwriting — the nod to Thomas Pynchon on "Sailing To Philadelphia," for example. How did your love affair with books begin?

When I was eight, I was ill in bed, and I was bored with all of my books, and I remember my mom giving me something by Steinbeck. She would also read poetry to me. Before that, I used to listen to a program called *Listen With Mother*. I was maybe two or three years old. It was on the radio every day. I think a lot of that appreciation for language starts when you're that young. This program was a mixture of music that was played for kids. I'd be listening to things like "The Big Rock Candy Mountain" and I would know all the words, but I didn't know what it was about. I didn't know what a hobo was (laughs). I just liked the sound of it.

I know a lot of musicians and songwriters feel that it's important to stay in touch with that innocent way of how they first responded to music, without worrying about if something is hip or cool.

Exactly. I didn't know what a country song was. My generation, a lot of us would've heard Ray Charles singing a country song without realizing it was a country song. It was just great. That's all that mattered. This is a link that goes back to Leadbelly and skiffle and Lonnie Donegan and stuff, in that we didn't care if a song was happy or sad. The tradition was that you needed a repertoire for different kinds of gigs, whether it was a medicine show or a party or whatever. When you're a child, you don't care if a song is happy or sad, you just like it for what it is. It's always interesting to me as a lover of songs to see that aspect of it. Like when you'd hear Hank Williams singing a sad song, the tempo would still be up.

Do you remember the first time you heard rock 'n' roll?

Well, I heard my uncle playing some boogie-woogie on the piano when I was about eight or nine, and I thought those three basic chords were the most wonderful things in the world. I still do (laughs).

You would've been twelve or thirteen when the Beatles hit. Was that a big event for you?

Of course. I knew about "Love Me Do" and I liked that, but "Please Please Me" made a bigger impression. That was in '63. But I was well away before that. I was gone. I was a lost cause before the Beatles (laughs).

Were you writing your own songs at that point?

No, that didn't happen until a few years later, when I was about eighteen. It was a gradual evolution from playing other people's music to finding my own style, my own voice. It's a synthesis.

How do you mean?

You have to expose yourself to a lot of music, then you have to play a lot. The advantage to playing a lot is that you play more and more like yourself. Your own style will emerge. But that only happens when you play *a lot*. If you just play a little bit, then you'll play pretty much like a lot of people.

That's sound advice for a songwriter.

The thing about songwriting is that there is no real formula to it. If I found a formula, I would definitely tell you and your readers exactly what it was (laughs). I think I'm just a bit of a gypsy, a rag and bone guy. I might have a fragment, but different songs come for different reasons. It's the bits of rag and bones that you pick up that can eventually make a song. But sometimes the song bell goes off, like "This will be a song" (laughs). Those kind of situation songs, where you literally find yourself in a place, and the circumstances combine and you're in a song situation. Other times, it could just be something someone says to me. A line that reverberates. Other times, it could be something from a book or a newspaper article. Inspiration comes from anywhere. I do find that other art inspires. Art makes more art. It's a wonderful feeling to be part of that, to inspire other people to do things.

There was a point when Dire Straits was one of the biggest bands on the planet. Did that kind of fame suit your personality?

No, I don't think it did it all. I'm not so sure whether it suits anybody's. I think I only just managed to cope with it. Not being a teenager made it a little bit easier. But still, it's pretty disruptive. At the same time, it's what I wanted (laughs). The fame is saying, "You wanted this."

Did it put more pressure on you as a writer?

It was slightly strange, in that suddenly you're this professional who's written a hit, and you're expected to write more. It can lead to a certain amount of negativity, being exposed to the music business all of a sudden, as opposed to music. They're two different things.

What's the most satisfying aspect of making music for you?

To be able to write a couple of decent songs, and to make a decent record, that's all I really want to try to do. I'm really enjoying my writing these days, and my recording, so I feel very fortunate indeed. If I don't get up on a stage in front of people for a while, I get a bit antsy to do it. So that's always been an aspect of it too. With Emmy being the same, I guess that's why we're doing this little tour. Real people in an audience have always been a part of it for me.

Any final words?

I think a big part of songwriting is being awake and alive and responsive to life. Eventually something of your own will emerge. Songwriting to me is endlessly fascinating to me because it's mysterious, because there is no formula. I don't think I could sit down in a Brill Building situation and write that way. But then again, I think there's an awful lot to be said for putting yourself behind the guitar, to put yourself in the position where you're actually make some music. The guitar is only going to write a song when it's out of the case.

Mark's Essential Listening:
There aren't really specific records, but I think Bob Dylan has been the most important for me, just in terms of falling in love with songs. It has a roots-based thing to it, and a poetic aspect to it. A record like *Blonde On Blonde*, when I was about fifteen, was everything to me.

The Dixie Chicks: In the Line of Fire

They've taken their hits and now the Dixie Chicks hit back with what may be the best adult pop CD of the year. Er, will anyone buy it?

By Josh Tyrangiel
With Andrea Sachs
From *Time*

Natalie Maines is one of those people born middle finger first.

As a high school senior in Lubbock, Texas, she'd skip a class a day in an attempt to prove that because she never got caught and some Mexican students did, the system was racist. After Maines joined the Dixie Chicks, and the Dixie Chicks became the biggest-selling female group in music history—with suspiciously little cash to show for it—she and her bandmates told their record label, Sony, they were declaring themselves free agents. (In the high school that is Nashville, this is way worse than skipping class.) Now that she's truly notorious, having told a London audience in 2003, on the eve of the Iraq war, "Just so you know, we're ashamed the President of the United States is from Texas," Maines has one regret: the apology she offered George W. Bush at the onset of her infamy. "I apologized for disrespecting the office of the President," says Maines. "But I don't feel that way anymore. I don't feel he is owed any respect whatsoever."

A sizable chunk of their once adoring audience feels the same way about the Dixie Chicks. After Maines' pronouncement, which was vigorously seconded by bandmates Martie Maguire and Emily Robison, the group received death threats and was banned by thousands of country radio stations, many of which still have informal bans in place. The Dixie Chicks have mass appeal—you can't sell 10 million copies of two of your three albums without engaging lots of different people—but country radio is an indispensable part of how they reach people. Programmers say that even now a heartfelt apology could help set things right with listeners, but it's not happening. "If people are going to ask me to apologize based on who I am," says Maines, "I don't know what to do about that. I can't change who I am."

As proof, the first single from the Dixie Chicks' new album, *Taking the Long Way* (out May 23), is called "Not Ready to Make Nice." It is, as one country radio programmer says, "a four-minute f—you to the format and our listeners. I like the Chicks, and I won't play it." Few other stations are playing "Not Ready to Make Nice," and while it has done well on iTunes, it's quite possible that in singing about their anger at people who were already livid with them and were once their target audience, the Chicks have written their own ticket to the pop-culture glue factory. "I guess if we really cared, we wouldn't have released that single first," says Maguire. "That was just making people mad. But I don't think it was a mistake."

Whether the Dixie Chicks recover their sales luster or

not, the choice of single has turned their album release into a referendum. *Taking the Long Way's* existence is designed to thumb its nose at country's intolerance for ideological hell raising, and buying it or cursing it reveals something about you and your politics—or at least your ability to put a grudge above your listening pleasure. And however you vote, it's tough to deny that by gambling their careers, three Texas women have the biggest balls in American music.

Over lunch in decidedly uncountry Santa Monica, Calif., where they have lived part time while recording *Long Way*, the Dixie Chicks—in fancy jeans, tank tops and designer sunglasses—seem less like provocateurs than busy moms (they have seven kids in all, ages 1 to 5) amped up by a little free time. In conversation they are loud and unembarrassable, celebrating their lack of boundaries in that escalating, I-can-be-more-blunt-than-you way unique to sisters (which Maguire and Robison are) and women who have shared a tour-bus bathroom. They eagerly discuss the soullessness of Tom Cruise, the creepiness of Charlie Sheen and the price-fixing practices of hair colorists. But sex is the perennial champ, and they are in a constant state of speculation about which of their kids' nannies is most likely to "get some" on tour this summer. "We're all married," says Maguire, "so it's not like we're going to."

One product of their decade together is that the Chicks are loose with pronouns (they use I and we interchangeably) and agree on almost everything, although the ways they agree can be revealing. When the conversation turns to childhood pets and I mention a beloved one-eyed dog, they all make empathetic faces, but Maguire, 36, gets teary, Robison, 33, laughs at her sister's sensitivity, and Maines, 31, says she would have poked around the empty socket "just to check it out." On Iraq, Maguire begins, "The night we sent missiles over ..." while Maines prefers, "When we bombed the s— out of ..."

In the days preceding the March 2003 U.S. invasion, the Dixie Chicks were touring Europe. They don't subscribe to *Foreign Affairs*, but they are daily newspaper readers who back up their positions with a solid understanding of current events. It struck them as natural that in front of a largely antiwar crowd in London, Maines would preface "Travelin' Soldier," an apolitical ballad about a heartsick Vietnam G.I., with a reference to the world outside the theater. As Maines spoke, though, Robison admits, "I got hot from my head to my toes—just kind of this rush of 'Ohhh, s—.' It wasn't that I didn't agree with her 100%; it was just, 'Oh, this is going to stir something up.'"

The celebrity playbook for navigating a scandal is one word long: repent. But apologies are for lapses of character, not revelations of it, and sensing that they were being asked to apologize for their beliefs as much as their timing, the Chicks decided not to back down. "Natalie knows we could have totally convinced her to apologize," says Maguire. "But the fact is, any one of us could have said what she said." Their demure response to the bans and threats—one of which arrived with the date, time and method of Maines' planned assassination—was to appear nude on the cover of *Entertainment Weekly* with slurs (Saddam's Angels) scrawled on their naked bodies. That did not placate the offended. More fans and friends were lost. Gradually, though, the need for round-the-clock security faded.

Now when they talk about "the Incident," as they unfailingly call it, the Dixie Chicks try to write it off as an absurdity. Maines has powerful gusts of indignation and real disdain for a few right-wing websites and talk-show hosts, but what seems to linger most is disappointment in her pre-controversy self. "I think I'd gotten too comfortable living my life," she says. "I didn't know people thought about us a certain way—that we were Republican and pro-war."

With George Bush the official pieta of the music industry, the Dixie Chicks' ordeal should have cooled by now. "We struggle with that all the time," says Maguire. "Are we picking the scab of something that's already healed? Because we don't know what people are thinking." Radio programmers make it their business to know. "They're still through the floor," says Dale Carter, program director at KFKF in Kansas City, Mo. "There's a technology called the Dial where listeners react to songs, and every time we test the Dixie Chicks ..." Carter makes a noise like a boulder falling from a high cliff. "It's not the music, because we're playing them the hits they used to love. It's something visceral. I've never seen anything like it."

The unwillingness of audiences to forgive the band is inseparable from politics. Market research indicates the average country listener is white, suburban and leans to the right, and they need not lean too far to file away an insult against a wartime President. Still, as the President's support has eroded and growing numbers of Americans (presumably some country-music fans among them) have come to disapprove of both his performance and the decision to go to war, shouldn't there be a proportional feeling of forgiveness toward the Dixie Chicks?

Country Music Television (CMT) has conducted numerous focus groups on the band. "And they're all a great study in the American psyche," says Brian Philips, the channel's executive vice president. "What comes up over and over again is, 'It would have been one thing if they'd said it on American soil, but it's the fact that they said it in Europe that really sets me off!'" There's an accusation of cowardice in there—although Maines insists, "I said it there 'cause that's where I was"—but if the way Philips draws out the syllables in Europe is to be believed, there's also a more personal grievance, an uneasy cocktail of resentment and abandonment. As Tim McGraw, one of the few vocal Democrats in country, and the only major artist who would speak on the record about the Dixie Chicks, says, "You've got to remember this is a family skirmish, and it's possible there's more than one thing going on."

Country music has never been particularly classy, which is one of its principal charms. Less charming is its defensiveness about its station. Unlike rock fans, most of whom are attracted to the music's integration of styles, some country fans—particularly those who call up radio stations in a lather—take it upon themselves to patrol a wall of genre purity. Elvis Presley and Johnny Cash got passes because they were sui generis. Not so Buck Owens, who in 1965, after a few experimental dalliances, took out an advertisement with a career-saving loyalty oath, "Pledge to Country Music," in the *Music City News*, promising, "I Shall Sing No Song That Is Not a Country Song." Even now, acts that other listeners reflexively think of as country, from McGraw to Willie Nelson to Shania Twain, are often disparaged for keeping an eye on the Hot 100, playing non-country songs or showing a little navel. The message from hard-core listeners is, stay behind the wall.

Early in their careers, the Dixie Chicks did, and they were beloved for it. Maguire and Robison started the group in their teens (Maguire was then at Southern Methodist University; Robison never finished an application to the Air Force Academy) with two singers in their 30s before eventually replacing them in 1995 with Maines, a Berklee College of Music dropout who, at the time, was attending her third college in three years. After a lot of dues paying, the band took over the country charts. Maines has an immensely powerful voice, but she's also capable of barometric emotional adjustments; she almost never oversings and thus sounds great coming out of stereo speakers. Meanwhile, in a medium that values tradition, Maguire and Robison played the most traditional country instruments, fiddle and banjo, and played them well. It didn't hurt either that all three were lookers.

The Chicks have affection for their early work, and songs like "There's Your Trouble" and "Goodbye Earl" will endure, but Maines describes most of it as "amateurish." They didn't write their hits, and the songs they did write were mostly filler. "I never wrote anything from my point of view," Maines says. "Even if it was something that happened to me, I would write it like it was a character and I was telling someone else's story ... That's not very brave."

This is what talented musicians are supposed to do: aspire to get better, braver. But at each step of their evolution, from their feud with Sony (ungrateful!) to the bluegrass album, *Home* (not country enough!), and then, of course, the Incident, the genre's wrath hovered like a jealous boyfriend. "Their old audience feels a little betrayed, a little left behind maybe," says CMT's Philips. That may explain why, as the Chicks and country began their breakup, country fans ran into the arms of brilliant redneck instigator Toby Keith, who displayed a doctored photo of Maines and Saddam Hussein at his concerts.

It also explains why the Dixie Chicks have made such a point of saying good riddance. "I'd rather have a smaller following of really cool people who get it," says Maguire, "who will grow with us as we grow and are fans for life, than people that have us in their five-disc changer with Reba McEntire and Toby Keith. We don't want those kinds of fans. They limit what you can do."

When the group gathered in early 2004 to talk about a new album, none of the three sounded nearly that confident. "You could tell this thing had strengthened them personally but shaken them artistically," says producer Rick Rubin, famous for his work with the Red Hot Chili Peppers and Beastie Boys and on Johnny Cash's haunting *American* series. "What turned me on, though, was that even though people were divided over what they said, people cared what they said, and that's a very strong position for an artist to be in. For the first time the girls, these cute little girls, had a platform."

Rubin took on the project with the hope—he's way too Zen to make demands—that for the first time in their careers the Dixie Chicks would write all their songs, by themselves and about themselves. As writers they admit they're prone to laziness, like people at a gym who need a personal trainer to force them to concentrate. Gary Louris of the Jayhawks, blues artist Keb' Mo' and Dan Wilson of Semisonic were brought in to co-write and supply discipline, and the band hunkered down in Los Angeles, where Rubin lives, to begin the long and unglamorous work of crafting songs.

Most of the material that emerged over nearly two years of writing was about marriage and kids and modern life as the Dixie Chicks and lots of other people live it. Oblique references to the controversy made their way into a few songs, so Wilson suggested they write one that addressed the issue head on. "Natalie said, 'Does that mean we'd have to forgive the people that were so evil to us?' And I said, 'Maybe it does,'" Wilson recalls. "And with a little wave of her hand, she said, 'Nooooope.' Then the next morning that phrase 'I'm not ready to make nice' appeared."

The song builds to a massive crescendo under lyrics ("It's too late to make it right / I probably wouldn't if I could / 'Cause I'm mad as hell / Can't bring myself to do what it is you think I should") that are explicitly clear. Those who loathe the Dixie Chicks will never get to the end, while those who love them will listen once, say *Yeah!* and probably not need to go back.

It works better as a referendum than as a pop song, but as Robison says, "We wrote it for ourselves, for therapy. Whether or not other people think it was important enough to say, we think it was." Says CMT's Philips: "I hope the audience lets them get this out of their system, because it would be the musical crime of the century if people don't hear this album all the way through."

That's a bit much, but you probably won't hear a better adult pop album this year. Musically, *Taking the Long Way* is full of swaggering country-tinged rock hooks—like a peak Eagles record, except without the misogyny and drug references and the advice to Take It Easy. Instead the songs aspire to do what the best pop always does, function as a smart expression of its creators' lives while remaining accessible to its listeners'. There are allusions to the recent past—on the jubilant opener "The Long Way Around" ("It's been two long years now / Since the top of the world came crashing down") and the breakup song "Everybody Knows" ("I swore they'd never see me cry / You'd never see me cry") — but they're only obvious if you look for them. "Bitter End" is a sing-along about fair-weather friends (the group fell out with a few lefty rockers who, amazingly, felt cheated of the nation's opprobrium) and even Lullaby is the rare song about kids well crafted enough that the childless could mistake it for a love song. And as things begin to sag a bit in *Long Way's* final third, the album delivers a knockout, "So Hard," the first pop song in memory about infertility (Maguire and Robison conceived by in vitro fertilization) and also the catchiest, most complicated love song on the record.

Will anybody buy it? The Dixie Chicks talk about *Long Way* as the end of their commercial salad days, but they're shrewd enough to know that only suckers choose between art and commerce. "I'm not ready to fly coach," jokes Maguire, and indeed *Taking the Long Way* could easily sub as the title for their marketing plan. They'll tour starting in July and flog the record on a few select talk shows. "Natalie's new motto is, 'What would Bruce Springsteen do?'" says Robison, laughing. "Not that we're of that caliber, but 'Would Bruce Springsteen do *The View*?'"

They're not doing *The View*.

Maines says she's not looking for more battles, but she won't shy away from any either. "Everything was so nice and fine and happy for us for the longest time," she says of their pre-Incident days. "It was awesome to feel those feelings again that I felt in high school: to be angry, to be sure that you're right and that the things you do matter. You don't realize that you're not feeling those feelings until you do. And then you realize how much more interesting life is."

It Was the Singing— A Conversation with Mac Wiseman

By Thomas Goldsmith
From *Bluegrass Unlimited*

Mac Wiseman may be the ultimate bluegrass insider.

Years before bluegrass was even called that, the great Virginia-born singer was one of a small group of musicians, picking and singing this music at the beginning. Along with Bill Monroe, Lester Flatt, Earl Scruggs, and a few others, Wiseman helped define bluegrass for all time, nearly sixty years ago.

Yet, Wiseman is by no means living in his illustrious past. In the last year or two, as he's rounded the curve of 80, he's recorded as a guest with the likes of Johnny Cash and Charlie Daniels. And he maintains a steady, though limited, touring schedule. Perhaps most notably, Wiseman recently recorded three CDs worth of the great old songs he loves to sing.

"Mac puts so much into it," Charlie Daniels, a fan for many years said. "His voice is still so good. It's amazing."

Jesse McReynolds, of the foundational duo Jim & Jesse, another musician whose career goes back to the early bluegrass days, worked on the forthcoming CDs. The sessions were filled from Wiseman's capacious song bag of patriotic numbers, old ballads, and gospel tunes. "He was singing as good as ever," McReynolds said.

In Wiseman's case, "as good as ever" means he's reaching the mighty standard he set beginning in the 1940s. His vocal performances stood out then as now, as somehow mellow and piercing at the same time, with every word clearly pronounced and hit dead-on pitch. Emotion and knowledge of his mostly down-home subject matter spiraled out of the grooves of those old 78s. Fans and, later, bluegrass critics have followed him through the decades. As long ago as 1965, the folk-music magazine *Sing Out* cited Wiseman's "gentle sweetness."

They call him the "voice with a heart," but Wiseman is anything but a softie. His intellect, humor, and perspectives on music and life have always been sharp and sometimes biting. Bobby Cudd, a highly regarded Music Row booking agent who worked with Bill Monroe in the '80s, remembers when he was trying to assemble a tour that would put the finest acts in bluegrass in some of the country's best venues. But having Monroe at the top of the bill meant that Cudd had to walk through a minefield of bluegrass feuds and loyalties. "He was almost like my consultant," Cudd recalled of working with Wiseman. "I'd call him up and say, 'Mac, do so-and-so and so-and-so have any trouble working together?'"

Not too long ago, Wiseman sat and talked at a restaurant in the Nashville suburb he laughingly calls L.A., for Lower Antioch. As waitresses hovered and tourists dined, he told stories about the small and great figures of bluegrass and country, stories about his colleagues, fans, and friends. The giants of this music, many of them departed, come alive and walk through Mac Wiseman's stories.

It Was the Singing: A Conversation with Mac Wiseman

"Three years ago, I was sitting at the house. The phone rang and it was John," he said, speaking of Cash. "He sent a driver and car for me and we went out to his cabin back in the woods where he had his little studio. It was a chilly October night and we just sat there and reminisced and got reacquainted.

"You know how I start my day, every day?" Wiseman recalled Cash saying. "I listen to your recording of 'Reveille Time in Heaven.'" Cash and Wiseman wound up recording "Reveille Time in Heaven" and Cash's song "I Still Miss Someone." Then June Carter Cash, Cash's beloved wife, died on May 15, 2003.

"After June died, I wanted to call him, but I didn't know what to expect. Two weeks after June died, he called me." Again, Cash sent his car for Wiseman and again they recorded favorite old material. Cash's producer, rap/rock kingpin Rick Rubin, had given him license to record whatever he wanted: gospel songs, Hawaiian songs, cowboy songs. They were joined in the studio by a small cast that included Cowboy Jack Clement and Laura Cash, the fiddler who's married to John Carter Cash. "We recorded 'Hold Fast To The Right,' that song that both our mothers taught us. When we did 'Hold Fast To The Right,' I'd always done it in G, and he did too, but an octave lower.

"By God, a few weeks later, he was gone." The recordings with Cash and Wiseman aren't out. They're part of a large store of Cash recordings yet to be parceled out, but Wiseman has heard that they have been mastered, or sonically prepared for release.

In early 2005, McReynolds answered the call to accompany Wiseman in the studio. With Wiseman on guitar and vocals and McReynolds on mandolin, they started work, and just kept rolling. "I did about thirty songs with him," McReynolds recalled. "Mac had these old songs he had learned through the years and he wanted to get them down on tape."

Wiseman originally wanted to do an album of all patriotic songs. "It started going so well that we also did old ballads and gospel songs," he said. "We cut 33 masters, enough for three CDs, in 13 or 14 hours over five days."

Asked about it almost half a year later, McReynolds recalls pretty much hanging on for the ride. "We sat down and he went through them pretty fast," he said, still struck by the high quality of Wiseman's singing at age 79 (he turned 80 on May 23, 2005). "It was really a fun thing to do. I'll say one thing though. Everything I know is on this album. I did all the intros, all the backup. I did a lot of the split-string stuff, crosspicking ..."

At his festival performances (he does 16 a year), Wiseman uses much of his show for an even more stripped-down presentation: just voice and guitar. After a few songs with a band, he goes it alone. "I just sit there with the guitar and visit with them and explain the old songs," he said. From his seat on the festival stage, Wiseman can see audience members nodding and smiling at the low-keyed approach, historical context, and old-time memories that he brings to the show. It usually comes in the midst of a line-up of high-powered, high-volume acts, many of whom Wiseman says he knows are good, but can barely distinguish from each other.

"They say they can hear it," he said of audience response to his set. "I do songs like 'Silver Dew On The Bluegrass Tonight,' 'Tonight At Nine,' and 'Drifting Too Far From The Shore.' I might do four gospel songs in an hour. I'll sit there and do one song and it'll remind me of another. I'll do 'Mary Dear' and 'There's A Star Spangled Banner Waving Somewhere,' then 'Boys In Blue,' 'Lorena.' I'll do 'White Cliffs of Dover.'"

It Was the Singing: A Conversation with Mac Wiseman

In another recorded appearance, Wiseman shows up along with Earl Scruggs and members of Del McCoury's band on the recent Charlie Daniels' CD *Songs From The Longleaf Pine*. Native North Carolinian Daniels, 69, was in his teens when he first tuned into Wiseman's music.

"I followed Mac I believe from when he first started recording," said Daniels, who's best known for his work in country-rock. Wiseman was a natural choice when Daniels started gathering musicians for his bluegrass gospel CD. "It was like eating Sunday dinner with a bunch of old friends," Daniels said.

At one point, former Foggy Mountain Boys bandmates Scruggs and Wiseman were at the studio at the same time. Not wanting to impose on Scruggs' time, Daniels asked his wife and manager Louise Certain Scruggs if it would it be all right if they recorded something with the historic line-up. "Mac suggested 'Keep On The Sunny Side'," Daniels said. "Earl just kicked it off," said Mac.

"On the way home I got to thinking, I had not been in the studio with Earl in 56 years. It was in the fall of 1948 with the Foggy Mountain Boys, their first sessions in Knoxville." Again, it's clear that Mac Wiseman isn't resting on his distinguished laurels. Like his venerable peers Scruggs and B.B. King, he's out there doing what he does best. Yet, he tells the old stories graciously, his eyes shining with the memories of those days.

"Lester and Earl came to find me," he said of his 1948 stint with Flatt & Scruggs. "I had been on the radio in Bristol, Va., just me and guitar. I couldn't figure out what they wanted from me. And then I realized it was the singing."

Jim Eanes sang with Flatt & Scruggs for a week or two early on, but after that, Wiseman held down the second guitar and tenor vocal slot for some historic months. The lineup with Wiseman started out at radio station WHKY in Hickory, N.C., home of their original fiddler Jim Shumate, but found it slow-going there. "I told them, 'I know that Bristol territory inside and out,'" recalled Wiseman, who had worked previously at Bristol's influential station WCYB. That's where the Foggy Mountain Boys started making real headway as a band. "We opened on a Thursday on WCYB and played three gigs that weekend," Wiseman said.

The popularity of WCYB meant that bands who played there had ready access to a circuit of live performances that was their real livelihood. Wiseman recalled that he enjoyed every minute of his association with the Foggy Mountain Boys. They were to make some historic recordings for Mercury Records, but not before a little known interlude that brought an offer from a legendary record label chief, King Records' Syd Nathan.

"King offered us a deal and wanted us to do the Monroe stuff," Wiseman said, noting that Nathan made a practice of having artists imitate the most successful acts on the market. "He had Hawkshaw (Hawkins) doing Tubb. In 1947, he wanted me to do Monroe material. I knew I'd never get anywhere as a copy."

Wiseman said he talked Flatt out of the deal, arguing that Flatt & Scruggs should record using their own, increasingly distinctive style. "Flatt really wanted to go with King. He wanted to show Monroe he could get going fast." Instead, Flatt and Scruggs signed with Mercury. The result was that memorable 1948 session in Knoxville.

"A famous tune from that session was 'We'll Meet Again Sweetheart.' We did 'Cabin In Caroline' and 'God Loves His Children.' "I'm Going To Make Heaven My Home" rounded out the session, which featured Shumate and bassist Howard Watts in addition to Flatt, Scruggs, and

It Was the Singing: A Conversation with Mac Wiseman

Wiseman. It wasn't the first recording session for Wiseman, and it would be far from his last.

"I had recorded in 1946 with Molly O'Day," he said. "In 1949, I was on the last Columbia sessions with Monroe, where we did 'Can't You Hear Me Callin.'" Bill Monroe's sharply developed ear for talent had singled out Wiseman in the days when Mac had a solo act on WCYB, or so Wiseman learned from Flatt and Scruggs. "Monroe used to sleep in the car all the time. But Lester said Monroe would say, 'When we get up close to Bristol, wake me up. I want to hear that boy sing.'"

After the Foggy Mountain Boys formed, Monroe once offered Wiseman a job, right on the air, when Monroe was making a guest appearance with Flatt & Scruggs. It ticked Flatt off, Wiseman recalled with amusement some 57 years later. After Wiseman left Flatt & Scruggs around the end of 1948, he did take a job with Monroe in 1949, joining a Blue Grass Boys lineup that included bluegrass legend Don Reno on banjo and fiddler Floyd Ethridge. "I liked him very much," Wiseman said of Monroe. "I felt like I knew him as well as any one person could know him. We roomed together on the road." The lonesomeness of Monroe's music was very much a part of the man, Wiseman said.

"He was very introverted as a child because he was astigmatic. One of the things he talked about was when Charlie (Monroe) and one of the other brothers were working in the refinery business near Chicago. Eventually Bill, the youngest, was the only one of the three brothers not working. "Charlie and the other brother (Birch) would go with him to the office and pick up his paycheck, then they'd just give him an allowance."

When Wiseman joined Monroe, the days were long gone when Bill worked alongside brothers Birch and Charlie, then just with Charlie in the Monroe Brothers. It was Bill Monroe as head honcho, working toward a style based on his own musical and personal intensity. "I don't think to this day that he set out with a theory or a way to go," Wiseman said, growing thoughtful as he remembered that fertile period. "He was just doing his thing and doing it with a drive he couldn't do with Charlie.

"In his first bands, he didn't have a sense of direction. He didn't say, I am going to create bluegrass music." I give him credit for sticking to his guns. As far as being a founding genius, he did it, but without any intention. He had that drive."

Wiseman agrees with those who think that Monroe found the perfect musical complement in Scruggs, who had "just the thing that Monroe needed to feed off." Blue Grass Boys membership kept changing, and in October of 1949, an all-star cast recorded "Can't You Hear Me Callin'" Monroe, Wiseman, Rudy Lyle on banjo, Chubby Wise on fiddle, and Jack Thompson on bass. The song's lonesome lyrics, keening fiddle, and unearthly harmonies nailed its place as one of the greatest bluegrass recordings. Its title has showed up as the title of a Monroe biography and more recently as the name of an eighty-song CD set of bluegrass and bluegrass-related recordings. "I think that was the first bluegrass session recorded in Nashville," Wiseman said. "It's noteworthy if it's true."

Wiseman worked his way into a successful solo career after leaving Monroe, scoring hits on everything from "The Ballad Of Davy Crockett" to "Jimmie Brown The Newsboy," from "Shackles And Chains" to pop songs like "One Mint Julep" and "Scotch And Soda." Though he's thought of as a pillar of bluegrass, he still feels resentment that his career got narrowed by music-business discrimination against bluegrass as a style.

"What I did was accepted as country music," he said of

It Was the Singing: A Conversation with Mac Wiseman

his solo career starting in the 1950s. "I got as much airplay as Marty [Robbins], coast to coast. The terminology 'bluegrass' got its hand in my pocket. When that terminology came along, the radio stations cut it off like a spigot. Their image of bluegrass was Monroe and Ralph Stanley."

Between Wiseman's vibrant career today and his stories of the genesis of bluegrass, there are many more recollections of years in between. He spent years as an executive at Dot Records: "Sometimes I think I business-manned myself out of the damn business. I found myself doing $5-an-hour typing when I should have been doing $50-an-hour thinking."

He was a founder of the Country Music Association and the Reunion of Professional Entertainers. He teamed up with his old friend Flatt for the classic Lester and Mac albums of the 1970s. Through Scott Rouse, he got involved in the Groovegrass recordings, which combined bluegrass and dance music. "I was one of the first that believed in Scott Rouse's concept enough to do it," he said.

Instead of fading, Wiseman's career seems to be building up steam in its 62nd year. He's getting attention in publications like the alt-country bible *No Depression*. Major awards appear to be in the air as well. "I don't know where the momentum is coming from," he said. "We're getting calls from Manitoba, San Diego, the Northeast. The curiosity about this music is there. I can see it when I play these colleges. Sometimes people will come up and introduce their kids and say, 'This man came to my college (or my grade school), in the 1970s.'"

It's late in the afternoon at Shoney's. Waitress shifts are changing, as Wiseman reflects with understatement that he's seen some changes in the business he's served so well for so long. These days, he travels in an RV to carefully selected dates, earning critical acclaim and strong audience response. Mac Wiseman is still creating great new music, just as he has for more than six decades. Still, it's a long way from the hard early days of bluegrass.

"I never had a bus. We were always in cars," Wiseman said. "If you had had a bus, often there was no damn road you could drive it down."

Carrie Underwood's Wild Ride

By Peter Cronin
From *CMA Close Up*

In the year since she beat out blue-eyed soul shouter Bo Bice to emerge victorious as the 2005 American Idol, Carrie Underwood hasn't had a whole lot of time to savor her victory. As demanding and life-changing as the *Idol* experience was for Underwood, it was only a small taste of what was to come as her life became an endless series of press interviews, TV appearances, photo shoots, award shows, concerts and coast-to-coast travel.

And then she made a record. Released in November 2005 and propelled by its chart-topping leadoff single, "Jesus Take the Wheel" (six weeks at No. 1), Underwood's debut album, *Some Hearts*, quickly became the fastest triple-Platinum female country debut in history, spending a phenomenal 15 weeks at the top of *Billboard's* Top Country Albums chart. No doubt about it: for this 23-year-old singer from Checotah, Okla., the past 12 months have been one wild ride.

"I think the only word that I can say is, Wow!" Underwood enthused at a recent triple-Platinum celebration thrown by her label, 19 Recordings / Arista Nashville.

There's a lot to celebrate. Underwood's is the kind of out-of-the-box success that hits Music Row every once in awhile, boosting percentages and providing the country format with a much-needed shot in the arm. In other words, everybody's talking about Underwood. They may be debating her pop leanings or her reality-TV beginnings, but there's one thing they all say: This girl can *really* sing. That is made crystal clear with every one of Underwood's incredibly poised and pitch-perfect live performances.

While she's glad her contest days are behind her, Underwood is quick to give some of the credit for her "overnight" success to the sink-or-swim ethic of *American Idol*.

"It was basically like a boot camp," she said. "There was nobody to tell me what I should sing, or what to do, and being away from my friends and family, pretty much on my own, I had to grow up. If I could survive that and not go crazy then I could survive everything that followed. It *so* prepared me for what I do now."

Immediately following her *Idol* win, Underwood was hustled into the studio to record the contest-winning power ballad, "Inside Your Heaven." The single debuted at No. 1 on *Billboard's* Hot 100 singles chart and became the best-selling song of 2005. While the track displayed her stunning vocal chops in a big pop setting, Underwood insisted on recording a vocally challenging Martina McBride classic for the B-side.

I think 'Inside Your Heaven' is a good song, but I didn't choose it," she stated. "That's why we put 'Independence Day' on the back, because we don't want to confuse everybody. I like to try new things, but I'm a country girl and that's the kind of music that I made it clear I wanted to sing."

"Carrie from the very beginning always made the point that she was a country singer," said Sony/BMG Nashville Chairman Joe Galante. "She took a risk by doing that because it's obvious that Simon Cowell is not a fan of the music—but that is who she is. She is going to have a long and successful career here—and that is going to be a big shot for everyone in country music!"

Growing up in a fairly typical but non-musical family in small-town Oklahoma, Underwood was nonetheless exposed to all kinds of music in all kinds of places.

"We'd take car trips and my parents always had it on the oldies station," she said. "I got a lot of Rolling Stones, Creedence Clearwater Revival, John Denver and all that. My sisters were teenagers when I was growing up and they were in their rebellious stage, so I got a lot of '80s rock music out of them. But being from Oklahoma, country music was always playing everywhere. In every store you went into, if there was a radio on, 95 percent of the time it was a country station. So it was something that had a lot of influence on me."

Songs "Jesus Take the Wheel" and her latest single, "Don't Forget to Remember Me," are powered by Underwood's undeniably pure country sensibility, but deeper album cuts "We're Young and Beautiful" and "Why He Cheats" showcase the singer's more mischievous and sassy side.

"I think that has to do with what I grew up with," she said. "Dann Huff, who was one of the producers of my album, without me saying anything said, 'Do you listen to a lot of rock music?' And I said, 'Yeah, I like it.' And he was like, 'I can tell. A lot of choices you make vocally are choices that a person with a more rock edge would choose.'"

She may be comfortable with her rocking side, and she does possess one of those voices that can go just about anywhere, but when it came time to decide where she wanted to make her music, where she *lived*, for Underwood there was no hesitation.

"I'm sure a lot of meetings were held to try to figure out

a way to market me," she said. "But my management company made it very clear that I was going to sing country music and that's what I wanted. I love all kinds of music, but I feel like I fit with country and that's the kind of music I love."

Preparing to record her debut, Underwood went directly to the heart of Nashville's creative songwriting community. Her management team set up a "retreat" at Nashville's Karian Studios, giving Underwood a chance to mingle and even co-write with some of Music Row's biggest hitmakers. Songwriters Brett James, Hillary Lindsey and Rivers Rutherford took the time to get to know the person behind the image and custom-crafted songs to reflect Underwood's life and concerns, including one she co-wrote about her hometown.

"I wanted to meet the songwriters, get to know them and let them know the kind of album I wanted to make," Underwood said. "They broke off into little groups and I'd bounce around from room to room and give suggestions and sing part of what they'd written. We even recorded some rough drafts right there in the studio. 'I Ain't in Checotah Anymore' came from that time, and I co-wrote on another one that didn't make the album. I can't wait to get into the next one. I want to have a bigger hand in it and co-write on a lot more songs."

Underwood has also been busy touring and getting to know her fellow country artists, gaining some valuable advice along the way.

"The advice most people have given me is to take it all in," Underwood said. "Don't just go and go and go and not have fun with it. You've got to have fun."

As hectic as things have gotten, Underwood is definitely enjoying the trip, and she makes a point of taking regular breaks, heading home to Checotah and to her alma mater, Northeastern State University in nearby Tahlequah, where she recently graduated magna cum laude and where she still loves to spend time with her old, reliable, pre-*Idol* friends.

"I try to get home about once a month, so it's not that bad," she said. "I miss my family and my animals, but they're always waiting for me when I get home. And a lot of my friends still go to college in Tahlequah, so I'll go hang out with my sorority sisters for a few days. The people that knew me before, still treat me the same ... but when we go out it's a different story."

As she reflects on all she's learned and experienced in the past year and gets ready to head to Nashville to perform at the CMA Music Festival in June, Underwood has her country music priorities perfectly straight.

"I like the intimacy of the studio and hearing how everything evolves from the demo to the finished product," she said. "But there's nothing like being in front of the fans. Especially now, they come to see me, and they give off a great energy. They're happy to be there ... and I'm happy they're there."

Peter Cronin

Matraca Berg: Pensive Behind the Pen

By Robert L. Doerschuk
From *American Songwriter*

Nashville's Universal Publishing Building tops the city's scale for songwriting luxury. Its lobby is a symphony of polished hardwood and Victorian detail. From here, climb the staircase to the second floor, take a couple of turns, push through a big oak door, and you're inside a comfortable space, surrounded by framed, black-and-white photos that helpfully suggest musical themes—a saxophone, a tight shot of a violin. The fixtures are brass, the couches are smooth black leather. A digital keyboard idles near tall, sun-flooded windows.

Even so, Matraca Berg, one of this company's prize writers, rarely sets foot in here, except on afternoons such as this, for an interview or a meeting. As far as creating new songs, that happens at home, once the dog is walked and the coffee brewed.

This is just one of the many ways in which Berg doesn't fit the mold. She is, for one, local by birth. Star-eyed scribes come here from far and wide, each one dreaming of connections they'll make with mentors who will help them find their niche. Berg had exactly the opposite experience: The great writers streamed toward her, or more specifically to visit with her mother, Icie Berg, a session singer, song plugger, and writer known for her hospitality.

Matraca hit the jackpot a lot younger than most of her colleagues. At eighteen, she co-authored "Faking Love," which T. G. Sheppard and Karen Brooks sent to the top of the singles charts. And then, at this moment of her triumph, she did precisely what almost anyone else in her position would not have done: She left town to play in a boyfriend's band in Louisiana.

That was some twenty-five years ago. Since then, she has come back and staked her place within Nashville's most elite community of writers. In fact, if that torrent of songs that has coursed through Music Row over these past fifty-odd years could be channeled down to an essential trickle, we would find the best of Matraca Berg among them, gleaming like flecks of gold.

Only a few of her peers—Felice and Boudleaux Bryant, Harlan Howard, Kris Kristofferson, maybe three or four more—have exerted an influence as deep and enduring. And apparently she's just warming up. She remains prolific. She still appears in writing circles, waiting her turn alongside wide-eyed newcomers. And unlike most of them, when Berg unveils something new, the people who matter listen carefully.

People like Keith Urban, Trisha Yearwood, Martina McBride, Pam Tillis, the Dixie Chicks – practically every star whose sun has risen to the sound of her songs. Berg has recorded her own work as well, though it's been seven years since her last CD. A new one is underway, but that's not a priority; even as a little girl, she knew that her world would center on the pen, not the stage.

"My mom hung out with people like Sonny Throckmorton and Red Lane," Berg says. "Red used to put

Matraca Berg: Pensive Behind the Pen

nursery rhymes to music and play them for me at the kitchen table; he'd make up the melodies as he went. Kris Kristofferson, Mickey Newbury, Bobbie Gentry: I knew all them all as I was growing up. They were my heroes. I wanted to *be* them."

Their songs captured her imagination: "I could sing Mickey's 'Sweet Memories' when I was in kindergarten," she says. "'Ode to Billie Joe' was a big one to me. 'Sunday Morning Coming Down' … but 'Yesterday' was the first song that made me cry, even though I was too little to know why."

Her first song came one morning as her father was driving her somewhere. "He was a graduate student in physics at Vanderbilt," Berg explains. "He had some of these big sheets of really thick paper that they used in the computer room, on the passenger side of our car. I started singing in the backseat, making it up as I went, and he wrote it all down."

From that modest beginning Berg began writing songs as other girls might scribble in journals. Her lyrics drew from life, as they do to this day. For a while she thought about becoming a journalist or an actress, but really, there was never any doubt that songs were her passion. And she wasn't shy about playing them either.

"By the time I was out of high school I knew plenty of people who wouldn't ask me to leave when I showed up with my guitar," she says, following the thought, as she often does, with a throaty, feather-light laugh. "So one day Bobby Braddock heard me at a party. We were passing a guitar around, I played a song, and he said, 'You know, we should write a song together. You're good, especially for your age.'"

They came up with "Faking Love" and Berg's reputation soared. Overwhelmed by the sudden attention, she fled to Hammond, Louisiana, and spent a couple of years gigging around the state with the Kevin Stewart Band. "I sang and played keyboards—badly," she remembers, smiling. "But I missed Nashville, and my mother, terribly. I was young enough to still have very strong ties to her, so I burned up that highway between us many times, and it was a long drive."

As her mother's health failed, Berg moved back to care for her and, after Icie's death, to raise her younger brother and sister. She also kept writing, and singers kept asking for more. Tanya Tucker made "Girls Like Me" the title cut of her album in 1986, and Reba McEntire took "The Last One to Know" to number one the following year. Joe Galante featured Berg on the second volume of RCA's songwriter series in '88. Two years later she released her own debut, *Lying to the Moon*, with a single, "Baby, Walk On," that climbed into the top twenty.

It's easy to go on like this, listing Matraca Berg songs that have turned gold. But that's not the real story: The content of her work matters more than the numbers. And the secret to their success lay in her ability to draw from two often incompatible qualities: the commercial and the personal.

This wasn't an entirely new concept; Kristofferson infused his songs with poetry and honesty, at no apparent expense to his well being. But no matter who records "Sunday Morning Coming Down," no one can erase its identity as a Kristofferson classic. Berg's creations, by comparison, attained similar levels of eloquence, struck equally deep emotional chords, and yet surrendered themselves to all who could interpret them on their own terms.

To Berg, this just comes naturally. "We're all human beings," she says. "In our core—Dolly Parton calls it 'the God core'—we're the same. You don't have to try to write about your experiences in a way that will help other people relate to them. I used to do that. In fact, when I wrote 'Strawberry Wine' I was sure nobody could relate to it because it was so autobiographical, right down to the farm. I just thought, 'I'll have to record this myself because nobody else will.'"

Deana Carter did, though, and her recording helped it earn CMA's blessing as Song of the Year in 1997. It also confirmed the wisdom of seeking inspiration in real life, which is more likely to touch listeners than something more artfully contrived. "When I try to be poetic or romantic or dark, it just sounds like bullshit," Berg says. "But if you're committed to your song being what it's supposed to be, it seems to work itself out. Just write and, like a little gift, it'll come out eventually."

Milestones—the comings and goings of friends and teachers—helped bring Berg to the point of trusting that the lessons of life can nurture the creative process. "Harlan died, and Waylon died, and so did John and June, and something happened to me. I wanted to honor them and to explore the simplicity and dignity of what they'd done. I also wanted to challenge myself, because I was writing the same song over and over for a while: up-tempo, woman power, whatever. And so I began writing songs like 'I Ain't Lovin' You Today.'"

That song, Berg says, differs from most of hers in that she knew immediately who should record it. "Usually I never think about that when I'm writing, but after I finished this one I was on the phone, saying, 'Gretchen Wilson needs to hear this. She's the only woman in town that can sing it.' I've been wrong about casting, but I knew in my heart that this one was for her. I wrote it in the car, in the middle of a hectic day. I think my husband Jeff and I had a spat that morning. I was also missing Harlan really bad. I swear, the title just popped into my head, I wrote it down, and I felt like Harlan was sitting there with me."

Harlan Howard was one of a few collaborators that Berg credits with helping to find her voice. "I wrote with him in my early twenties," she remembers. "Harlan pretty much took the bull by the horns. You try to get a word in, but he was so incredibly fast, and that was intimidating to me because my process is very slow. Further down the road, in '99, we wrote some good stuff, when I was older and I wasn't afraid that he'd kick my ass. But he was just as fast and sharp as ever, and I just had to paddle and keep up.

"I loved working with Ronnie Samoset too," she continues. "We're kindred spirits. We were both struggling when we began writing together, and he was so encouraging that I felt comfortable for the first time going deeper into my experience, as opposed to just writing a hit song. And Gary Harrison is amazing. He's extremely fast, almost like stream of consciousness. He grabs this legal pad and goes at it, and then he rips out a page and hands it to me, and I'm like, 'Oh, what do we have here?' It's almost like he channels stuff. I especially love his turns of phrase. When we wrote 'Strawberry Wine' he came up with 'the fields have grown over now, years since they've seen a plow.' That just blew my mind. It brought tears to my eyes because it was so dead-on."

By focusing inward for her ideas, Berg admits to cutting herself off from some aspects of the business. "We've become much more corporate," she says. "Marshall Chapman once said that for writers, Nashville in the late sixties and early seventies was like Paris in the twenties. It was beautiful. I lived it vicariously through stories my mother would tell. Writers had more of a vagabond/poet thing going back then. Of course, they were crazier too. They'd get drunk and pick each other's songs. They didn't come to work if they didn't want to. So it was more dysfunctional than it is now, but the songs were really good."

With this, Berg glances wistfully out the door, down the hallway that's lined with other doors that lead into other rooms with digital keyboards and musical décor. "I mean, look at this building," she says. "We've got cubicles now. People come here to write from nine to five every day. They're hardworking craftsmen. They go home to their children at the end of the day. They make a decent living. It's more of a challenge, though, because radio wants *Up With People* all the time—lots of tempo.

"I'm no good at that," she says, with a smaller, despairing laugh. "A lot of younger people tell me that they dreamed of coming to Nashville back when Steve Earle and Nanci Griffith were going on. And when they got here it was gone. That makes me sad. But some great songs still slip through. So I guess there's a tradeoff."

Robert L. Doerschuk

GEORGE JONES

In a career that spans more than 50 years, George Jones talks about his life today and his new album, Hits I Missed ... And One I Didn't, scheduled for a September release

By Danny Proctor
From *Music City News*

At 74, he's considered by many as the greatest living country singer and has received nearly every honor imaginable, including two Grammy Awards, induction into the Country Music Hall of Fame in 1992, and the 2002 National Medal of Arts honor from President George W. Bush, the nation's highest honor for artistic excellence.

Originally conceived as "songs I wished I had recorded," Jones recorded 11 songs for the new album that includes many he had passed on over the years that went on to become hits for other people. The one hit he didn't miss is the first new version of his biggest hit, "He Stopped Loving Her Today," which was originally released in 1980.

The cuts include Willie Nelson's "Funny How Time Slips Away," Bobby Bare's "Detroit City," Alan Jackson's "Here In The Real World," Mark Chesnutt's "Too Cold At Home," Merle Haggard's "Today I Started Loving You

Again," and a duet with Dolly Parton on Hank Williams Jr.'s "The Blues Man."

George Jones chatted with Music City News about his new album and his life today.

The album is such a pleasure to listen to. Those classic songs are such a part of our music history and it's so great to hear you sing them.

Well, thank you. Those songs are just down to earth and hit so many people. That's what so great about traditional country music. Everyday working people can relate to it—or even if you don't have a job. (laughs)

It used to be a standard practice for artists to cover other singers' hit songs on their albums. If Marty Robbins had a hit, then Connie Smith might record a version of it. That doesn't happen anymore.

No, there's too much competition today, to tell you the truth. Usually, when a song is out by someone and it's hittin' for that artist, I would be too scared to cover it today. The thing about the old days is when you would cover somebody's hit—like Webb Pierce covered my first hit "Why Baby Why" back in 1956. He was well-known at the time and I was on a dinky label in Houston, Texas, and that was my first record. Our distribution wasn't good and a big name artist could take you over, back in those days. Nowadays, the way the business works, it doesn't make any difference what label you're on as long as you've got a good company that has good distribution.

Your duet with Dolly Parton on "The Blues Man" is great. The lyrics sound like they could've been written about you

in the first place—"started drinkin', took some things that messed up his thinkin' ... got cuffed on dirt roads, got sued over no shows."

Most everyone thinks it was written about me, which might be why I never recorded it before. That part of my life is not something I've ever been proud of. I think Hank Jr. probably had me, his dad, and himself in mind when he wrote it. The reason we did that song is that I always thought it would work best as a duet and Dolly agreed. So I said, "Hell, let's do it." It's not like we're covering Hank Jr. We're just doing a good song the way we think it should have been done. We did a little video thing together and I hope they're going to put that out before too long. Maybe we can get the right kind of exposure with this song. I hope so. It's hard to believe that Dolly and I had never had a duet before. She and Emmylou Harris sang with me on "Where Grass Won't Grow" on my *Bradley Barn* album but that wasn't a duet. I think Dolly shines on "The Blues Man." If Dolly and I were just 20 years younger, country radio would give us a big ol' hit, but now, who knows? In our hearts we know we have a hit.

Mark Chesnutt was thrilled that you included "Too Cold At Home" for the album. He's your biggest fan.

Well, that was one of the hits I missed. There are two or three on the album that I turned down. You have good days and bad days and it was one of those days when my listening ear wasn't listening too well. So, that was the idea, especially when we decided to record "He Stopped Loving Her Today" again for the first time in 25 years. I was going to call the album *Everybody's Hits but Mine*, but when we re-recorded that one over, the girls at the label thought we ought to change it to something else so we came up with *Hits I Missed … And One I Didn't*. It's hard to beat another artist who has had a big hit record on those songs. It's hard to re-do a song as good as you did it the first time.

So the label, Bandit Records, is your own?

We went in together with Evelyn Shriver and Susan Nadler and formed a little ol' label and it's really cooking right now. We don't have any artists except myself but we're hoping to get the financial part built up so we can sign other artists. The girls are very smart and really know what they're doing. They've been a lot of help and have kept my career going. All you have to do is keep cutting good records and get 'em to the people who want to hear 'em. I've got so many good fans who have stood by me for my entire career, plus a lot of new young fans. It's great to still be able to have those fans. At my age, I'm one of the very few lucky people to have that.

You wrote your autobiography I Lived to Tell It All **back in 1996. Since then, you've lived through some pretty tough times, including that awful car wreck.**

We sure have. It didn't look like we were going to do much after that. Lord, I have prayed—and I don't know why but He's kept me here for a purpose and I thank Him every day for it.

I've got the best fans in the world. They love my style of traditional country music and we don't have a lot of that today. They still want to hear it and come to see me and people like Haggard. Alan Jackson is still country and I'm surprised that they'll play him and George Strait who are traditional but won't play anybody else. But they're good-looking guys and they cater to the younger listeners. I guess that's how they can get by with staying traditional. I'm real proud of 'em. I hope they can continue and keep some of that alive because it's going down the drain in so many directions. I love Dierks Bentley and Brad Paisley and I enjoy being around 'em. They're doing a great job and they're good boys. I did the song "Cornography" on Brad Paisley's new album with Little Jimmy Dickens, Dolly Parton, and Bill Anderson. It's really funny. Jimmy Dickens is so funny.

I love that Brad includes a lot of humor in his music. You used to do that too with songs like "White Lightnin'."

We need to cheer this business up a little. It's getting too serious. We need more upbeat stuff. If I had my preference though, I'd rather sing a sad song that has a strong meaning. But I love to do the up-tempo things too because you have a lot of fun with them and your show on stage doesn't get too draggy.

I heard you and Loretta Lynn tell a story about riding down the road and singing sad songs to each other.

Yeah, she'd sing and I'd have another drink and cry. Then I'd sing one and she'd cry. You know, the good ol' days were fantastic. I wouldn't trade one of 'em for anything in the world, except for the bad days. But you know, everybody's life has to have the bad with the good. I wouldn't trade my experiences. I've finally learned to live the kind of life that I think people need to live. I finally realized that and I'm doing it and I'm enjoying the business so much more. They say "birds of a feather flock together—I lost a lot of them birds when I stopped drinkin—but I've got a lot of new friends and I'm really enjoying them.

Your daughter Georgette has a new album. I know you're proud of her.

Oh, yeah. We're gonna do some things together. She's a sweetheart.

Your website talks about an album you're working on with Willie Nelson.

We went into the studio and did three or four things but it's been hard to work out. We started it but haven't finished it yet. I haven't heard from him in a while. He's been busy filming *The Dukes of Hazzard*. I'm not into all that acting stuff. I do enough acting playing Possum.

How did you get into the George Jones Country Sausage business?

Some friends of mine, the Williams family here in Tennessee, asked me to join them. They've been very successful on their own so we thought we'd put my name on there and so far it's been doing fantastic. We're in about 10,000 supermarkets now.

You've received so many awards and honors. As a kid back in Beaumont, Texas, did you ever think you'd be considered the greatest singer in country music?

All you can do is dream of those things and I had my dreams. Thank God, a lot of them came true. You want things and you love something so much like I loved traditional country music. All I wanted to do was sing. I didn't even know they paid you. Then I found out that came along with it too. It was the greatest thing that could happen to me. I never thought I'd ever meet my first idol, Roy Acuff. Then it came about that I was sitting in a room and talking to him, knowing that I had been listening to him on the radio since I was a little kid about 4 or 5 years old. To think I'd ever meet somebody like that was out of the question. That's part of those dreams that you get fulfilled sometimes in life. It sure is a wonderful feeling and makes you so happy.

The last line of your biography on your website, www.georgejones.com, reads: "The Possum" is at a great place in his life and, for the first time in his adult life, is straight, sober and having the time of his life." Is that pretty accurate?

That's what I'm enjoying about life today. It's so different and not like a jungle and all mixed up the way it used to be. Hell, you've got a clear head, you know? You're not abusing your body anymore. You're making your life last longer. The different friends that you have now. It's just a beautiful world now.

Danny Proctor

TO BEAT THE DEVIL: INTIMATIONS OF IMMORTALITY (KRIS KRISTOFFERSON)

By Bill Friskics-Warren
From *No Depression*

Call the world if you please "The vale of soul-making...." I say "Soul making," soul as distinguished from intelligence. There may be intelligences or sparks of the divinity in millions, but they are not souls till they acquire identities, till each one is personally itself."
— John Keats, "The Vale of Soul-Making"

Am I young enough to believe in revolution?
Am I strong enough to get down on my knees and pray?
Am I high enough on this chain of evolution to respect myself and my brother and my sister,
To perfect myself in my own peculiar way?
— Kris Kristofferson, "Pilgrim's Progress"

To go in the dark with a light is to know the light.
To know the dark, go dark. Go without sight.
And find that the dark, too, blooms and sings.
— Wendell Berry, "To Know The Dark"

The life and songs of Kris Kristofferson have often inhabited the shadowy vale to which Keats and Berry refer — a liminal zone between darkness and light where souls are born and where, in the best of cases, they thrive. Sometimes the pursuit of these twilight reaches comes to a tragic end, as in "Casey's Last Ride" and "Billy Dee," songs in which Kristofferson's characters seek in vain "to satisfy a thirst [they] couldn't name." Other times the chase for this indistinct horizon can be bracing, as in the heady yet weighty rush of freedom in "Me And Bobby McGee." Maybe nowhere has Kristofferson given clearer voice to this liminal pursuit, though, than in "To Beat the Devil," a talking blues inspired by an early encounter with a wraith-like, self-medicating Johnny Cash.

The narrator of "To Beat the Devil" is an archetypal Kristoffersonian troubadour trying to find himself. Staving off a hunger that runs much deeper than his craving for whiskey or beans, he seeks refuge in a tavern on "Music City Row." There he not only confronts the shadows that await him (his own and those of the devil he meets), he embraces this veil as if it were his friend. Relishing the possibilities for transformation at hand, Kristofferson's scuffling protagonist matches wits with the devil and — just as Jacob did after wrestling all night with the phantom at the river's edge — emerges, if not with a blessing, then at least with a song to feed the hunger in his soul.

Kristofferson has long sought the shadows in the service of soul-making. As a singer, songwriter, actor, and activist — as a man — he's greeted the perils and promises inherent in those murky precincts as "provings of the heart," to borrow Keats' evocative phrase—as portals to self-discovery.

"Those shadows definitely challenge and test you,

To Beat the Devil: Intimations of Immortality (Kris Kristofferson)

whether you're up to it or not," Kristofferson said by phone from his home in Hawaii in December. "And you definitely learn from the tough ones. It's funny. Bucky Wilkin, who used to be in Ronny & the Daytonas and was with my first publishers, told me one time that if you took shadows and the devil out of my songs there wouldn't be anything left. I think maybe freedom, too."

Kristofferson added this coda about freedom with a chuckle, but he couldn't have been more serious. Early on he feverishly extinguished light after light, throwing away one bright prospect after another — breaking every tie, as he puts it in "Border Lord," before any of them could bind him.

He cast aside careers as a Golden Gloves boxer and as a Special Forces Captain and helicopter pilot in the Army. He turned down a cushy gig teaching English at the U.S. Military Academy at West Point. He squandered the respect and support of his parents, as well as the love and devotion of his wife and two young daughters. He chucked it all—comfort, security, prestige—for a move to Nashville, a ramshackle apartment, and drudge jobs as a bartender and janitor on Music Row.

And, of course, for a song, and with it, a shot at writing some for the ages. Which he did, forever changing what country music could say and how it could mean. Kristofferson, however, didn't just create a neo-Romantic prototype for Nashville tunesmiths; making his way sightless but with abundant imagination, he wrote the restlessly self-surpassing song of himself. Pursuing a persistently penumbral path to perfection, he took every "wrong" direction, as he sings in "The Pilgrim: Chapter 33," in the process of finding himself on his sometimes lean, often lonely, ultimately transformative way back home.

Ain't You Come a Long Way

Over the course of his prodigious career, but especially during bleaker times, Kristofferson has taken comfort in a maxim of William Blake's: "If the fool would persist in his folly he would become wise." This Blakean sense of completion or arrival, of a wayward pilgrim come full circle, is evident throughout Kristofferson's new album, *This Old Road*. The record's spiritual generosity, disarming sincerity, and unvarnished arrangements are reminiscent in places of both June Carter Cash's *Press On* and Neil Young's *Prairie Wind*. Equal parts autobiography, gratitude inventory, and rule for living, Kristofferson's short, sweet album is, in terms of emotional, social, and historical reach, his most realized to date.

Singing in the gnarled Sprechgesang that only in recent decades has begun to sound commensurate with his years, Kristofferson looks back on his wild-eyed early days in Nashville, "roaring" with the likes of Roger Miller, Willie Nelson, Mickey Newbury, and Harlan Howard. He thanks Lisa, his wife of 24 years now, for teaching him the meaning of love. He ponders the sanctity of life and how, inexplicably, people habituate themselves to death. The entire album is infused with an abiding sense of wisdom gained through struggle, the sense of someone "approaching perfection," as Kristofferson sings in "The Final Attraction."

And yet not perfection smugly or arrogantly conceived, but that born of grace, humility, and a fierce awareness of finitude. *This Old Road* is Kristofferson bearing witness to how, in his peculiar crucible of shadow and folly, he has forged a soul.

"I got lucky, I got everything I wanted / I got happy, there was nothing else to do," he sings, to a bounding melody recalling that of "I Walk The Line," in "Pilgrim's Progress." This bit about having nothing to do but get happy is anything but glib. Hard-won and then some, it testifies to the singleness of purpose that it takes to make any life work. And not only that, but to the overwhelming sense of gratitude that Kristofferson feels for having had a shot at such happiness — for "the freedom and the chances," as he says elsewhere on the album, "and all the truth and beauty [he's] been shown."

"I'd be crazy," he goes on, rounding out the chorus of "Pilgrim's Progress," "not to wonder if I'm worthy of the part I play in this dream that's coming true." Once again—and with lines that echo "Why Me"—Kristofferson isn't referring to the dream in question as if it's some passive fantasy that's happening to him. He's talking about the formation of something real that he has labored, by dint of folly and imagination, his entire life to create. A dream incredibly vivid and intense, and one that has encompassed so much. The triumphs and disappointments of a lifetime; a staggering array of collaborators and friends; the flowering of a radical political consciousness; a family once lost, now found; and lately, some heady recognition, including induction into the Country Music Hall Fame in 2004 and a retrospective of his movies at the South By Southwest festival in March.

"Look at that old photograph, is it really you?" he marvels to open *This Old Road*. Set off by Don Was' roomy production, the track's rustic strains of piano, harmonica, and mandolin lend a suitably hymnal cast to the mix of wonder and weariness in Kristofferson's craggy, pitch-indifferent whisper. It's the lassitude that lingers, especially when, after remarking to himself, "Ain't you come a long way down this old road," he sings of "running out of time," of "holy night...falling," and of "faces that [he's] passed along the way."

Many of those faces are now gone, including those of

peers and running buddies like Miller, Newbury, Howard, and Silverstein — and, more recently, Waylon Jennings. Easily the toughest goodbyes that Kristofferson has had to say of late, however, were those he bid Johnny and June Carter Cash, just four months apart, in 2003.

"God, I miss them," he said when the Cashes came up in our conversation, and they often did. "I look back on all that time that we spent together. I just wish that I had cherished every moment even more. But I feel so grateful to have known them as well as I did.

"That's kind of a presumptuous thing to say, you know? But to be close to them....," he went on, before pausing, maybe thinking the better of going too far down so intimate a path.

"Coming to town, you know, John was my idol," he began again, tracing a still personal yet ultimately more public arc. "I was just thinking the other day. One of the things that I like best about my life is looking at some of these people who were my heroes who became my friends. Like Willie and Waylon, and Muhammad Ali. But John was really special."

Cash, after all, befriended Kristofferson when he was still just a wannabe songwriter emptying ashtrays and running errands at Columbia Studios on Music Row. And it was the Cashes who, after inviting him to a dinner party at their home, asked Kristofferson to join them onstage at the Newport Folk Festival in 1967 — and who practically had to drag him up there with them after he'd hitchhiked all the way from Nashville to get there.

Cash, in an interview I did with him at the Carter Fold for *No Depression* a year before he died, still had vivid memories of his protégé's Newport debut. "When it came time for him to go onstage, I said, 'Kris, you go out and do whatever you feel like doing, then call me back out and I'll come back on,'" Cash began. "So it came time for him to go on and he stood there frozen. He couldn't move. I said, 'Kris, the emcee's calling you,' and he still couldn't move. He couldn't speak. He was petrified. Well, finally, June walked up to him, kicked him in the seat of the pants, and said, 'Get out there.'

"So he went out and he did 'Sunday Morning Coming Down' and 'Me And Bobby McGee.' I forget what else he did, but the next day, on the front page of *The New York Times*, it said, 'Kris Kristofferson Takes Newport.' I was really proud of that for Kris. He really needed that break; it was a great leap forward, and he got a really good one there."

Maybe not as big a break, though, as the one Kristofferson got from appearing on Cash's primetime variety show two years later. Or from Cash scoring a #1 country hit with the unexpurgated version of "Sunday Morning Coming Down" that he performed on his show in 1970.

That record would become Kristofferson's first chart-topping cut as a songwriter and would win him the award for Song of the Year at the CMAs. It also opened the door, as has been widely chronicled, to his shaggy, inebriated reception of the honor at the Ryman Auditorium, ensuring him Outlaw status a few years before anyone thought to give the iconoclastic persona he helped create a name.

The Burden of Freedom

The scene that Kristofferson made at the 1970 CMA Awards was hardly an anomaly. In many ways he had been crossing lines and taking risks, even to the point of self-sabotage, for much of his life. And maybe as a matter of course.

Along the way he had lettered in football and soccer at Pomona College and been a Golden Gloves boxer. He'd been inducted into Phi Beta Kappa and been a Rhodes

Scholar at Oxford. He'd won fiction contests sponsored by *The Atlantic Monthly*, and, as a young military officer, trained as a member of the Army's elite Airborne Rangers. The pressure — as an athlete, student, writer, and serviceman — to perpetually surpass himself must have been overwhelming at times.

Kristofferson's accomplishments were a great boon, to be sure. Yet being blessed with such a profusion of gifts — and with the privilege to pursue them so freely (his father was a two-star General in the Air Force) — must also have been a burden. A legacy that had to be lived down or shrugged on occasion, or at least be put in jeopardy every now and then for it to mean or be worth anything at all.

Why else would Kristofferson, with the constitutional impulsivity of someone with attention deficit disorder (how, in hindsight, could he have focused on any one thing?), discard the innumerable opportunities that his many gifts afforded him? Why, at times, would he go so far as to risk his life to feel more fully alive?

The most unforgettable and perilous cases of this habitual risk-taking were those, while stationed in Germany, when Kristofferson and his fellow pilots would get bombed and fly into the hollows of the Rhine River Valley, skidding along the surface of the water.

From picking fights in bars to jumping out of combat planes, though, Kristofferson's persistent shadow dancing was all of a piece. For much of the first 30 years of his life he had followed a well-lit, over-achieving path in keeping with his parents' status and respectability. Yet as rife with prospects as that well-heeled life might have been, it never really fed the gnawing in his soul. As a young man who'd been given so much and done so much with it, Kristofferson was still searching, as Mary Gordon would write of Jane Austen, for a sentence to fit him.

To Beat the Devil: Intimations of Immortality (Kris Kristofferson)

In Kristofferson's case that sentence would be a song, not a novel — and later, on occasion, a script. But whatever was going to fit, it was going to have to be something that didn't come easy and that wasn't encumbered by the weight of societal or familial expectations. It would have to be something, even if it cost him everything — and maybe because it would — where the only burden would be freedom. This burden of freedom is precisely what he's getting at in "Me And Bobbie McGee" with the gloriously double-edged line, "Nothin' ain't worth nothin' but it's free."

There certainly was a whole lot of nothing, and much of it onerous, after Kristofferson, then on the verge of turning 30, turned down that teaching appointment at West Point and moved to Nashville to pursue his songwriting muse in 1965.

Not that the move was without invitation. Marijohn Wilkin, the writer of such classics as "Waterloo" and "The Long Black Veil," was starting a small publishing house on Music Row. Acting on a tip from a relative who saw Kristofferson perform in Germany (as "Kris Carson" he'd previously cut some unreleased sides for the British pop impresario Tony Hatch), Wilkin signed him, along with the left-of-center likes of Chris Gantry and Johnny Darrell, to her fledging company, Buckhorn Music. The demo tape that prompted the deal was, as Wilkin recalled in a 2003 interview with writer Michael McCall, "a mix of Shelley and Keats set to the tune of Hank Williams."

The trouble was, Kristofferson's highfalutin' hybrid wasn't where country radio's collective head was at back in 1965. Buck Owens' sprightly "Before You Go"— a terrific though by no means Keatsian single — was the most successful hit on the Billboard country chart that year. Novelties like "Girl On The Billboard" and "May The Bird Of Paradise Fly Up Your Nose," as well as MOR ballads by

Nashville Sound perennials like Jim Reeves and Eddy Arnold, also predominated.

Roger Miller's "King Of The Road"— #1 for five weeks that spring — might have augured the progressive movement to come, but it clocked in, with Hemingway-like economy (and abundant comic relief), at just over two minutes. It would still be a few years before radio would be ready for Kristofferson's rambling mix of abstract and concrete, of shadows, devils, castles and whatnot.

A&R reps on Music Row weren't interested, in any event, in pitching Kristofferson's aphoristic musings to the acts they represented, and the few cuts that Wilkin did place weren't exactly hits. The first, a recitation of Kristofferson's "Talkin' Vietnam Blues" by the DJ and TV host Ralph Emery, didn't even break into the Top 100 of Billboard's country singles chart. Much the same fate befell the version of "For The Good Times" that producer Jerry Kennedy recorded with a female singer whose name nobody seems to remember anymore. "The Golden Idol," a 1966 single of Kristofferson's that Wilkin talked a head-scratching Billy Sherrill into releasing on Epic, stiffed as well.

In all fairness — and as Wilkin readily points out — Kristofferson had yet to calibrate the blend of highbrow and lowbrow that would become his stock-in-trade. He had some things to learn, or rather unlearn, before country audiences, the singers as well as the fans, would relate to his songs. "He had been a poet and an English teacher, so his songs were too long and too perfect," Wilkin said. "His grammar was too perfect... He had to learn to write the way people talk. He did, too."

Indeed, and not just by peppering his narratives with colloquialisms like "ain't," "Lord," and "nothin's" stacked back-to-back. Kristofferson also developed an indelible melodic sensibility — a languid, circuitous lyricism — that

To Beat the Devil: Intimations of Immortality (Kris Kristofferson)

went well beyond the gutbucket, Hank-cribbed shuffles he hit town with.

Avid to surpass himself and his peers — and not just as a writer, but also as a dypso and a brawler — he doggedly persisted, plunging into the shadows and mortgaging his future, as he sings in following stanza from his new album, for a stab at immortality:

> *We used to drink about a bucket of booze*
> *To try and chase away the black and blues*
> *When it come the time to pay your dues*
> *We gave an IOU*
> *To the devil with a dirty smile*
> *Which he added to the growing pile*
> *Of the promises we mean to keep*
> *The day your dreams come true.*

All of which was met with the enormous chagrin of his duty-bound parents. "I remember," Kristofferson said with a laugh, "my mother saying that nobody over the age of 14 listens to that kind of music, and that it wouldn't be anyone we'd want to know."

And they didn't, even if that nobody was their son, and even if the "shitkickin'" music in question was the least of their concerns. Not having bargained for the hobo-song-writer life, Kristofferson's wife and high-school sweetheart Fran was as bewildered as everyone else, leaving him and taking the kids with her not long after he'd dragged them to Nashville to pursue his quixotic adventure.

"God it was hard on the people around me, like my family," Kristofferson said, looking back on this dissolute yet thrilling time of his life. Even his brother, who'd stood by him longer than anyone else from the past he'd abandoned, eventually flew to Nashville to see if he ever was going to come to his senses. The occasion was Kristofferson getting fired from his side job — the only one that really paid anything — flying workers to and from offshore oil rigs in the Gulf of Mexico. He'd been found slumped over the controls of his helicopter sound asleep, with the blades revving wildly above him.

In another helicopter incident, Kristofferson landed his chopper on the bluff above the Cashes' house on Old Hickory Lake to deliver a demo tape rumored to have included "Sunday Morning Coming Down." "When you're heading for the border," he'd later sing, "you're bound to cross the line."

Trying to Sing Up All the Soul in Sight

"I was so thirsty to be hungry to be an artist," Kristofferson said, with characteristic wryness, of his fevered pursuit of songwriting glory. "There were a couple of guys who were sort of the heroes of the ones of us who considered ourselves underground 'cause no one cut our songs. It would always be Roger Miller, Willie Nelson or Johnny Cash. Everybody just seemed to zero in on one, but I was the only one who liked all of 'em."

This omnivorous and insatiable appetite for inspiration, coupled with his exposure to a mind-boggling amount of great songwriting in so short a span of time, certainly served Kristofferson well. "I had to get better," he told Michael McCall. "I was spending every second I could hanging out and writing and bouncing off the heads of other writers."

Talking with me by phone in December, he said, "We took it seriously enough to think that our work is important, to think that what we were creating would mean something in the big picture. Looking back on it, I feel like it was kind of our Paris in the '20s. Real creative and real

To Beat the Devil: Intimations of Immortality (Kris Kristofferson)

exciting. And intense."

Pushing himself relentlessly, Kristofferson was living the Romantic ethic, the privilege and self-assurance to which he was born perhaps affording him the strength and resiliency to do so. He and his cohorts called the most intense of these times "roaring" — marathon sessions where they binged not just on music and smoke and drink, but on inspiration itself.

"We used to take about a day and a night, trying to sing up all the soul in sight," Kristofferson sings to the bare-bone, neo-rockabilly arrangement of "The Show Goes On:" "Anyone who couldn't see the light, we had to leave behind."

Yet after three years in Nashville that saw him leaving just about everyone he loved behind, the hits still weren't coming. Not only that, Kristofferson's contract with Buckhorn was up for renewal at the end of the year. Thinking that his songs might stand a better chance in other hands, he jumped to another publishing company, Combine Music. Owned by Nashville movers-and-shakers Fred Foster and Bob Beckham, Combine had a clutch of hungry young writers on staff, including Shel Silverstein, Mickey Newbury, Tony Joe White, and Billy Swan. Foster also owned Monument Records, without which Kristofferson likely wouldn't have been afforded the chance to record his raspy debut, easily the greatest set of "demos" ever assembled.

That album, monolithically titled *Kristofferson*, was still two years in the offing. For the time being, the most auspicious thing about Kristofferson's deal with Combine was meeting Mickey Newbury. A fellow Texan — Kristofferson was born in the border town (where else?) of Brownsville — Newbury didn't write by the numbers any more than Kris did, but at least he'd managed to get some of his songs cut.

The biggest by far had been "Just Dropped In (To See What Condition My Condition Was In)." The song's title was as outré and unwieldy as anything to come out of Nashville, but "Just Dropped In" became a Top 5 pop hit for the First Edition in early 1968, for better or worse jumpstarting singer Kenny Rogers' blockbuster career.

Inspired by Newbury's writing and encouraged by his friendship and example, Kristofferson finally — and in an elegant encapsulation of the code by which he'd been living to this point — found the sentence, "Freedom's just another word for nothing left to lose," that fit him. Just as crucial, it would also prove to be the sentence that put him over the top as a songwriter.

Newbury was with Kristofferson on a madcap flight across the country when he sang that line from "Me And Bobby McGee" for Roger Miller. From its hipster argot to its peripatetic narrative, the song sounded nothing like what people were playing on country radio at the time. But it was perfect for Miller, a boho-leaning eccentric whose mid-'60s rash of Grammys might have done more to make country cool with pop audiences than the trio of LPs that Bob Dylan subsequently recorded on Music Row.

Miller's version of "Me And Bobby McGee" only climbed as high as #12 on the country chart in the spring of 1969. It was enough, however, to give Kristofferson his first major hit as a songwriter, paving the way for an epochal streak that included four #1's over the span of just six months.

The first, which peaked the final week of June 1970, was Ray Price's tender, countrypolitan reading of "For The Good Times." Then, in September, came Cash's version of "Sunday Morning Coming Down." (Ray Stevens had cut the song, to little notice, in 1969.) Sammi Smith's heart-stopping transformation of "Help Me Make It Through The Night" followed in December. Three months into the

To Beat the Devil: Intimations of Immortality (Kris Kristofferson)

new year, Janis Joplin, with whom Kristofferson briefly was linked romantically, hit #1 on the pop charts with "Me And Bobby McGee" (in the wake of her death the previous October). All three of the country #1's also charted pop, with "Help Me Make It" reaching the Top 10 and "Good Times" stalling at #11.

Even more important than this commercial breakthrough, if inconceivable without it, was the way that Kristofferson, at this point in his mid-30s, revolutionized how people on Music Row thought about and wrote songs. Overnight, it seemed, he had infused country music with the sexual candor of soul music and the mystical-existential urgency of Dylan, the Beats, and his beloved Romantics.

Meditating on freedom and commitment, alienation and desire, darkness and light, Kristofferson's songs tapped down-home as well as countercultural vernacular, and with them, the prevailing Zeitgeist. Steadfastly refusing to talk down to his audience, he proved that country music could be both hip and grounded while speaking to the most fundamental of human struggles and emotions.

Maybe nowhere did Kristofferson achieve this more sublimely than with "Sunday Morning Coming Down", as vivid an evocation of being hung over as any ever written. At one level, the song shines a sobering light on the shadow side of roaring, of smoking your brains all night with cigarettes and songs and whatever else could be had for inspiration — and wondering, as Kristofferson puts it in "The Pilgrim," "if the goin' up was worth the comin' down." And yet the hangover depicted in "Sunday Morning" is as much spiritual and moral as it is physical; the estrangement felt by the song's protagonist — "nothing short of dying" — is devastating.

The sound of people singing in church, the smell of chicken frying, and the laughter of a father playing with his daughter all remind Kristofferson's protagonist of the places he might have been had he not been wandering the streets with a throbbing head, wishing he was stoned. These scenes clearly tweak his conscience, much as it must have stung Kristofferson to have cut himself off so completely from his family.

Still, and herein lies the rub, Kristofferson's narrator knows that he wouldn't feel any more at home in those putatively more nurturing places or situations. No less than in songs like "Rank Strangers" or "Stones In My Passway," the veil of loneliness and estrangement here — no mere state of mind — borders on the absolute.

Illumination, not judgment, is the byword here, and Kristofferson's gift for inhabiting such shadows, his willingness to venture into and search the darkness for enlightenment, is the key. It is his ability to find beauty even in utter loneliness that redeems it. Indeed, that makes it sing.

The Burden of Freedom (Not Just Another Word)

Kristofferson, of course, went on to become an enormous celebrity in the decade that followed. He had a prolific, if uneven run as a recording artist, both with his second wife, Rita Coolidge and as a solo act (his 1971 LP, The Silver-Tongued Devil And I, was certified Gold and his 1973 single "Why Me" was a country #1).

He also embarked upon a successful, if uneven movie career, including strong starring roles in *Pat Garrett & Billy The Kid*, *Alice Doesn't Live Here Anymore*, and Louis John Carlino's bracing adaptation of Mishima's novel, *The Sailor Who Fell From Grace With The Sea*. By the time he co-starred with Barbra Streisand in the 1976 remake of *A Star Is Born*, Kristofferson had become a strange mélange of Hollywood beefcake/millionaire, hipster renaissance man, and poet laureate of country music.

To Beat the Devil: Intimations of Immortality (Kris Kristofferson)

He also was still living hard, his drinking and drugging at times getting out of hand. His Hollywood exploits, including a spread in *Playboy with Sailor* co-star Sarah Miles, made for fecund tabloid fodder. Kristofferson was living in Los Angeles by this point and his life had begun to resemble the unmanageable one of the character he played (a self-fulfilling prophecy?) in *A Star Is Born*. Musically, he seemed out of touch, so much so that at the time Tom T. Hall said, "One of my favorite songwriters died of overexposure."

Kristofferson admitted as much in a previous interview with *No Depression*. "Whether it had been the movies or just the reality of being on the road," he said, "it would have cut in on some of the creative experiences that are in 'To Beat The Devil' or 'Sunday Morning Coming Down.' I wasn't living in that place anymore."

Kristofferson got something of a handle on his drinking as the '70s drew to a close. Perhaps due to this newfound clarity — "Chase The Feeling" from his new record seems to be born of those insights — he also got serious about writing songs again. Freedom had long been at the heart of his lyrics, but primarily as understood from a personal or artistic standpoint. Now, for the first time in any sustained way, Kristofferson's writing spoke to the meaning and implications of shared freedom, and especially, to the social and political burdens it entails.

Such discernment is a crucial part of the process of soul-making, and in this case, of becoming a self within the larger human community. "I get lazy and forget my obligations / I'd go crazy if I paid attention all the time / And I want justice but I'll settle for some mercy / On this holy road through the Universal Mind," Kristofferson sings, exhorting himself, in "Pilgrim's Progress." Sounding both a Buddhist and Jungian note with this reference to the "Universal Mind," he's talking about the archetypal journey to consciousness, the process of becoming a soul.

"There's a responsibility that comes with freedom to do what's morally right," he said, referring to the opening outward of his understanding of freedom during the interview we did together. "I was always writing what I was feeling. But the stuff that I was becoming aware of in the 1980s, the things that were going on in the world were important enough that they were something that I should be talking about. You know, what was going on down in Nicaragua and El Salvador."

The fruits of this increasingly political turn in Kristofferson's songwriting didn't surface on record until the release of his 1986 album *Repossessed*. In the song "What About Me" he took aim at the Reagan Administration's not-so-covert military operations in Central America. With the single "They Killed Him" he lifted up prophetic martyrs like Jesus, Gandhi, and Martin Luther King, each of whom died for standing up for what they believed.

Radio programmers weren't interested. "One guy said, 'The only thing wrong with killing Martin Luther King was they didn't have more bullets in the gun,'" Kristofferson told writer Peter Cooper in an interview that appeared in this magazine a year and a half ago. Record labels likewise grew wary; apart from his work with Waylon, Willie, and Johnny Cash in *The Highwaymen*, Kristofferson found himself relegated to the indie fringes.

Nevertheless, he persisted with this "folly," becoming more explicit in his denunciations of U.S. treachery and aggression — and in his embrace of Latin and African rhythms. Broadsides decrying greed ("Love Of Money") and hypocrisy ("Aguila Del Norte") appeared alongside anthems offering encouragement (the title track) and advocating moral responsibility ("The Eagle And The Bear") on his 1990 album *Third World Warrior*. Traces of liberation theology were evident as well, notably in paeans to solidarity like "Jesse Jackson." "He was marching next to Martin when he died," Kristofferson sings, "Working face to face in Cuba / And Managua, Nicaragua / He did not yet beat the devil, but he tried."

"Sad to say, it's even worse today," said Kristofferson, who included a song about an artist killed in a missile attack of Baghdad on his 2003 album, *Broken Freedom Song*.

"I can't help but be appalled at the arrogance of our behavior as a superpower — the superpower — to attack a sovereign nation," he went on.

"To attack, basically, a bunch of people because you disagree with what their leader is doing. If that's OK, then the rest of the world is going to be gunning for ours because they certainly don't like what our government's doing. And the people who are paying for it are the people that we're bombing. There's no way in hell we can ever make up to the people in Iraq what we've done to them. There's not been a time when I've been on the planet that I've been as depressed at the direction that our country's been going.

"And it's all being done in the name of God. It amazes me. It's a real holy war going over there and I really have no idea how it's gonna end up."

A new song of Kristofferson's called "In The News" speaks to this idolatrous equation of divine will and human agendas with particular eloquence — as well as anything since Buddy Miller's *Universal United House Of Prayer*, an album steeped in the wisdom and outrage of the Hebrew prophets. "Anyone not marching to their tune they call it treason," Kristofferson sings, "Everyone says God is on his side."

From here, just as he did in 1986's "Love Is The Way," Kristofferson goes on to portray God as an empathetic being who not only shares in human suffering, but who suffers at the expense of humanity's habituation to death. "Don't Blame God, I swear to God he's cryin' too," he admonishes, before shifting voices to God's. "'Not in my name, not on my ground / I want nothing but the ending of the war / No more killing or it's over / And the mystery won't matter anymore.'"

Pilgrim's Progress: The Last Thing to Go

The mystery that's at stake in "In The News" has fueled Kristofferson's quest to discover and define himself from the beginning. On his new album, he gives most explicit voice to it in "Holy Creation", a song steeped in a sense of the sacred inspired by Blake's contention that "Everything that lives is holy." Yet it's only with another song on *This Old Road*, "The Last Thing To Go," that Kristofferson, by way of a wry nod to his boxing past, links this mystery, which he ultimately identifies with love, to the burden and promise of freedom. "Love is the reason we happened at all," he sings, accompanied by harmonica and acoustic guitar. "It paid for the damage we'd done, and it bought us the freedom to fall into grace."

Kristofferson isn't talking about love as if it were just another emotion like lust or boredom that comes and goes with our moods. He's talking about love as a more pervasive — and maybe everlasting — force. A healing power that, more than just helping people make it through the night, makes freedom possible in the first place.

"Love to me is the only answer to what's going on with the world today," he said in December. "The kind of love I'm talking about is the kind that you feel unconditionally for your children. And if you work at it, you can get to where it includes others too. Which isn't as easy as it is with your children, but I think it should work there.

"In the people we've been talking about, like John and

To Beat the Devil: Intimations of Immortality (Kris Kristofferson)

June," he went on to say, referring to the Cashes' preternatural gift for embracing strangers and people on the margins, "it worked from there outward to where they could feel love for people they weren't even related to. If you were to attain the highest state, I guess you would love everybody."

The idea of reaching such an elevated state — yet another way of talking about soul-making — likewise derives from Blake. "He wasn't, like, into organized religion," Kristofferson was quick to point out, referring to Blake. "But he believed that if you didn't do your duty as a creative person to promote spiritual communion, your soul was lost for eternity."

In "The Final Attraction", the track that serves as the benediction on *This Old Road*, Kristofferson refers to the pursuit of this higher state as "approaching perfection" — an "intimation of immortality," as Wordsworth put it. Inspired while waiting in the wings as Willie Nelson went back onstage to close a show, Kristofferson sings,

> *Well, here you are*
> *The final attraction*
> *Awaiting direction*
> *From somewhere above*
> *Your final performance*
> *Approaching perfection*
> *I know what you're making*
> *Is some kinda love.*

"Somewhere in your lifetime" he goes on, now singing the song of himself — and others — to dusky filigrees of Dobro and acoustic guitar. "You were dared into feeling / So many emotions / That tear you apart / But they love so badly / For sharing their sorrows / So pick up that guitar /

And go break a heart."

This process of breaking a heart, one's own and those of others, is harrowing, and not just because it can be terrifying to dwell in the shadows as Kristofferson, trying to beat his devils, so often has done. This practice of breaking a heart, of being torn apart by painful emotions, is also harrowing in the more pregnant sense of the verb "to harrow" that has fallen out of usage — that of the often violent process of breaking into the ground and opening it up to prepare for new growth and eventual harvest. In Kristofferson's case, the process of breaking into the cold, dark recesses of the heart to cultivate a soul.

Kristofferson goes on, in "The Final Attraction," to enumerate some of the other pilgrims he's known, from Waylon Jennings to Mickey Newbury, who submitted to this harrowing process of soul-making. It's a gesture reminiscent of how he sometimes introduces his old standby "The Pilgrim: Chapter 33," the famous chorus of which begins, "He's a poet, he's a picker / He's a prophet, he's a pusher."

Kristofferson has said that this song began as a study of Dennis Hopper, only to become associated with Johnny Cash. And yet "The Pilgrim" also describes Kristofferson himself — indeed, any of his fellow sojourners who took every wrong direction on their often lonely way back home. Evocative of the overriding journey to consciousness at the heart of Kristofferson's life and work, "The Pilgrim: Chapter 33" has become something of a meta-narrative — words for living for all who go in the dark without sight to find that the dark, too, blooms and sings.

Buck Owens 1929-2006
Country legend put his fans first until the very end

By Tom Roland
From *Country Weekly*

Buck Owens always had the fans in mind, and that was true to the very last time he played.

On Friday, March 24, Buck showed up at his Crystal Palace theater in Bakersfield and ate chicken-fried steak for dinner. He wasn't feeling well and decided to call off his performance for the evening, but on the way to his car, some fans said they had come all the way from Oregon and really wanted to hear him. Buck changed his mind and performed that evening.

It turned out to be the final show of his career. Buck died in his sleep early the next morning from heart failure at age 76.

Buck was a colossal figure in country music, a 1996 inductee in the Country Music Hall of Fame noted for a string of hits such as "I've Got A Tiger By The Tail," "My Heart Skips A Beat" and "Act Naturally" that brought a driving energy to the genre.

But for many fans, his role as a co-host of the cornball *Hee Haw* series eclipsed his work as a musician. Buck's trademark red, white and blue guitar was a familiar presence on the weekly series that showcased country's top talent alongside quick comedy sketches. The show was lampooned by critics, but Buck recognized the levity it brought to the masses—and it didn't hurt that he said he was paid better for his efforts on the show than he'd ever been paid for music.

Buck certainly had an affinity for common folks. He grew up in *un*common poverty, born Alvis Edgar Owens in Sherman, Texas on August 12, 1929—just weeks before the stock market crash that signaled the beginning of the Great Depression. Victimized by the Dust Bowl, his family did the same thing that many others did in that era by packing up their belongings in November 1937 and heading off to California, 10 people stuffed into a sedan. Along the way, the trailer hitch broke, and Buck grew up in the Phoenix area as a result.

The family was so poor that he never owned a pair of new shoes until the year he turned eight and he didn't have a toothbrush—using cloth and soda instead—until he was 11. Two years later, he received a mandolin for Christmas and taught himself to play.

By the time he was 19, Buck was driving trucks by day and playing at night in the clubs, where he met Bonnie Campbell, who soon became his wife. In 1951, Buck moved to Bakersfield, where he became part of a robust club scene that also sprouted such acts as Merle Haggard (who married Bonnie after she divorced Buck), Wynn Stewart and Johnny Paycheck.

The clubs demanded a big sound, and Buck infused the same driving, raucous feel into his recordings once he got signed.

"I had more drums in mine—I *felt* more drums," he said. "I wanted country music to be a little more exciting."

Buck established himself as a session guitarist during the 1950s, appearing on recordings by Tommy Collins, Bobby

Bare and Wanda Jackson. On one of those sessions, record producer Ken Nelson convinced him to sign with Capitol Records, launching a career that would generate 47 Top 10 hits in *Billboard* magazine, including 21 that went all the way to #1.

Owing partially to his understanding of those working-class people who would hear his music on the radio, Buck wasted no time in building his songs. In hits such as "Together Again," "I've Got A Tiger By The Tail," "Love's Gonna Live Here" and "Waitin' In Your Welfare Line," Buck slammed the hook home early and often, making sure the listener could remember the music.

"Twenty seconds is all people need to listen to know if they like something or not," he theorized. "I've seen that happen. The producers, in just 24 seconds you can give them the whole song."

With his backing group, The Buckaroos, Buck was one of the hottest country acts of the 1960s, epitomized by a landmark appearance at New York's prestigious Carnegie Hall. Buck was a bit reticent to play the venue, believing Manhattanites would be unresponsive. But the show sold out and produced a live album that remains influential to this day.

"That's the one that turned me around, because the playing was so great and the singing was so incredible," says Ray Benson, whose western swing band Asleep At The Wheel has won eight Grammy awards. "Those close harmonies are just beautiful. Buck's songwriting's just classic."

In fact, Buck died on the 40th anniversary of that legendary show. In addition to the Carnegie concert, March 1966 was a turning point in two other ways: The Buckaroos started touring in a bus instead of a camper, and Buck bought Bakersfield radio station KUZZ. It became part of a business empire that would include numerous stations, particularly Phoenix's KNIX, which has won numerous awards within the industry.

KNIX was also influential on Dierks Bentley, who grew up in Phoenix, and came to appreciate much about Buck's approach to music.

"He kept his band small, but it really had a kick to it," Dierks notes. "If you look at my band, it's the same instrumentation—steel guitar, electric guitar, drums and bass, that's it. That's what Buck had. No fiddle—I don't have fiddle. And there's two-part harmony—I just have two-part harmony. It's that small band—looks like a rock band, but they're playin' country music, and he really made the band a part of the show. He's really influenced me that way."

A tragic change in Buck's band helped to alter his fortunes in the music business. Don Rich, the Buckaroos' guitarist and harmony singer, died in a motorcycle accident in July 1974. In later years, Buck admitted that he'd gone through extreme depression after Don's loss and that it adversely affected his music.

In 1980, Buck all but retired from performing, though Dwight Yoakam would influence a renaissance. Dwight publicly professed his admiration for Buck's music before the two had even met, and he gradually persuaded Buck to join him in recording "Streets Of Bakersfield," which became Buck's last hit in 1988. A year later, Buck teamed with Ringo Starr on a new version of "Act Naturally," which The Beatles had covered in 1965 and released as the B-side of "Yesterday," and the new version earned a Grammy nomination.

Buck had surgery for throat cancer in 1993, but after he recovered, 1996 turned out to be a huge year for him. Sherman, Texas, renamed a portion of Highway 82 the Buck Owens Freeway, he joined both the Country Music Hall of Fame and the Nashville Songwriters Hall of Fame, and he opened the Crystal Palace, where he played on a regular basis for most of his final decade.

In one of his last public acts, he unveiled 10 bronze statues celebrating country legends from Hank Williams to George Strait, and one of those legends, Garth Brooks, proposed to Trisha Yearwood on stage that same evening.

It was Buck who convinced Garth years earlier to buy his masters from Capitol Records, a move that eventually led to the deal Garth was able to strike with Wal-Mart last year.

But Garth was hardly the only artist that Buck influenced. Many younger acts sought his advice, and Buck gave it willingly.

"My friend Buck Owens was one of a kind, a larger-than-life music legend who reinvented country music, epitomized musicianship, and was the inspiration for countless artists, including the Beatles," said Brad Paisley, who wore Buck's Carnegie Hall jacket the night he joined the Grand Ole Opry. "He loved to become friends with other musicians and loved to pass advice on to young guys like me. He was very giving of his talents and wisdom.

"If any good can come from his passing," said Paisley, "I hope that it's a renewed interest in his achievements, and more importantly, his incredible Bakersfield sound. He deserves to be remembered as one of the most important artists in all of music history."

Tom Roland

Climbing to the Top of the Duo Heap

An Interview With Troy Gentry of Montgomery Gentry

By John Hood
From *Country Weekly*

Country music giveth and country music taketh away. Nobody knows that better than Troy Gentry, one-half of the multi-platinum selling duo, Montgomery Gentry. In the seven years he and partner Eddie Montgomery have been in the spotlight, they've seen countless other acts rise and fall, while they've slowly, steadily and relentlessly worked their way to superstar status. They've witnessed the short career arc of other performers first hand. That's why they continue to work harder, play more shows and work on their careers with more gusto than your average country star.

Montgomery Gentry's incredible work ethic has moved them into headliner status on the road and resulted in *Something To Be Proud Of*, a *Greatest Hits* album that also includes the current Top 10 single "She Don't Tell Me To." They're driven to be the best and, although the competition is friendly, Gentry admits they'd love to supplant Brooks & Dunn as the hottest duo in country music. With a new studio album scheduled for release in the fall and a multi-artist package tour in the planning stages, this just may be the year Troy and Eddie move to the head of the duo class.

Gentry recently spoke with *Music City News* about how their early career shaped their sound and he also gives a sneak peek at the duo's plans for 2006.

"We played a lot of clubs. We packed a lot of vehicles and whatever cars we owned at the time, loading them up with gear traveling from club to club trying to find places that would let us play," says Gentry of the duo's formative years before signing with Sony. "We worked odd jobs during the day trying to make the ends meet so we could play at night around Lexington and the state of Kentucky."

They also earned their performance stripes the old fashioned way, by getting in front of people and learning how to help an audience have fun. It was a lesson they learned quickly because their livelihood depended on it.

Gentry says, "We learned how important it was to interact with the people that came to hear us. We learned how to perform. People came out to the clubs to have a good time and be entertained. Back then if you didn't entertain the crowd and the crowd didn't come around, you wouldn't keep the job very long."

They hit Nashville with a ton of momentum but quickly realized it takes much more than good music to have a long career. Gentry says they studied successful artists who had been around awhile to try and figure how to stay in the game for the long haul.

"The guys we looked up to who were mainstays were the guys who were out there all the time working the road as much as possible," he says. "They stayed visible. When we first signed our deal and started traveling we figured the more we were out there the more visibility and notoriety we'd get. Those things lead to more radio play and record sales. We stuck to our guns on that and worked as much as possible. We didn't want the public or radio to forget about us and us go away like some acts have in the past."

No amount of hard work can make you a country radio star if you can't back it up with hit songs. From the very beginning Montgomery Gentry not only found great songs, they picked songs that encapsulated the duo's blue-collar, good-times attitude. Their first single "Hillbilly Shoes," a raucous country-rocker, put them on the map. They quickly followed with songs celebrating rural, working-class life ("Daddy Won't Sell The Farm," "My Town"), as well as cuts that summed up their fierce independence ("She Couldn't Change Me," "Hell Yeah").

"We listen to a lot of songs," says Gentry. "We've found a couple of writers like Jeffrey Steele, Chris Wallin and Rivers Rutherford who have a knack for writing things that we want to sing about. Back in the clubs we sang about everyday life whether it was good or bad. We focused on singing songs that people could identify with. It worked for us. Writers started realizing that what we were singing about was everyday life."

He also says the more success they've found, the easier it gets to find hit material. "There's an old saying in Nashville that the bigger you get, the better songs you get," he explains. "We've proven ourselves to be an act with mainstay that's going to be around for a while. As we grow as an act we're starting to get big writers and songs from the 'A-list' pitched to us."

The single and *Greatest Hits* album are red hot right now, but Montgomery Gentry learned a long time ago not to rest on their laurels. They're already hard at work on the next studio album.

"We've got six or seven tracks down and we go back in sometime in later this month to finish up the rest of it. We're looking at somewhere around an August release.

We've stepped up to the plate and found some incredible songs. We're getting better in the studio and with our singing. It's a lot of the same style stuff we've done in the past, but even more in-your- face."

They will also be touring heavily this year. They will headline fairs and festivals throughout the spring, but Gentry hints at bigger plans for a fall tour.

"Eddie and I have kind of wanted to do something a little different. We may look at another act from a different format to join up with us. We could introduce musical styles to each other's crowds. We might team with an old school classic rock band and maybe add something from a new, different genre of music—kind of our countrified version of Lollapalooza. We want to make something unique that people can get excited about coming out to see."

Whatever they come up with, it'll be another step on their way to the top of the country music mountain. And make no mistake about it; they want to be kings of the mountain. Even it means giving their pals Brooks & Dunn some friendly little help off the top of the heap when the CMA Awards roll around in November.

"Brooks & Dunn and Big & Rich and everybody else has their own unique sound and style of music," he says. "That's what's so great about the Duo category. It's not like we're competing for the same audience. We all bring something different to the duo thing. The category is getting more interesting with Big & Rich coming on and Blue County and the Van Zant brothers. It does get a little competitive. Big & Rich maybe sparked us since they came out. Eddie and I have been busting ass since day one. Each year as our career is getting better, we feel closer to overtaking Brooks & Dunn and would like to do it. So, yeah, there is a little friendly competition."

He also admits most of the competition happens around

awards show time. Then Montgomery Gentry gets back to what they do: entertaining their fans. "When the awards are over we forget about all that and get back to the important stuff," says Gentry. "That's getting out there and making good music and playing to the fans who buy our music and come listen to our stuff. That's the best reward of all."

That's the kind of attitude that helped Montgomery Gentry stay around long enough to put out a greatest hits album. When it comes to their career in country music, they've created something to be proud of.

John Hood

SONGS OF FAITH

More than ever before, songs about faith are making history on the country charts. But will the spirit last?

By Alanna Nash
From *Country Weekly*

Country music has always echoed the heartbeat of America and, down through the years, it's also echoed the spirituality of America, with songs such as Hank Williams' classic "I Saw the Light" and scores of other uplifting tunes, including Vince Gill's "Go Rest High on That Mountain" and Steve Wariner's "Holes in the Floor of Heaven." And as the events of the 21st century—9/11, the conflicts in Afghanistan and Iraq, and Hurricane Katrina—occupy so much of the nation's consciousness, a historic number of poignant songs of faith, grief, healing and, yes, God, are scaling the singles charts like never before.

"I can't ever remember this many songs on the charts that are talking about spirituality or whatever you would care to call it," notes Wade Jessen, manager of the country, bluegrass, Christian and gospel charts for *Billboard* magazine.

In the past 18 months, country radio has aired a record-setting 11 spiritually themed hits, with 10 of those coming in 2005. There are songs about friends and relatives in the afterlife, as in Kenny Chesney's "Who You'd Be Today" and George Strait's "You'll Be There." Brad Paisley has included gospel songs on past albums, and his recent No. 1 duet featuring Dolly Parton, "When I Get Where I'm Going," also contemplates the other side. And Carrie Underwood's "Jesus, Take the Wheel" and Brooks & Dunn's "Believe" offer hope for those who call on a higher power.

Brad Paisley reveals he recorded the heaven-oriented "When I Get Where I'm Going" because of events in his life. "My reason for cutting it had everything to do with my life, in that I lost my aunt a year and a half ago to cancer. This song really summed up the hope of everyone who's ever lost someone. I had no idea that this would be a hit song, I just knew it was important to me. I've heard of so many accounts of people who have adopted this song themselves and I'm really proud of that. It's a great feeling when something like this becomes larger than just my own personal tribute."

Brooks & Dunn's "Believe" began when songwriter Craig Wiseman told Ronnie Dunn he had an idea for a song that revolved around "I raise my hands / I bow my head." The two then got together to expand on the idea.

"Craig's style of writing is almost like channeling," notes Ronnie. "We sat down for two days, and we had a song. I went through religious school, and I'm always dealing with the polar opposites of spiritualism and tattoos and whiskey. I think this song gets its message across without preaching. It's not a religious thing. It's just like, 'Hey, there's something out there to hang on to when everything else has gone to hell.'"

Call it a sign of the times, but the trend toward songs of faith is a natural outgrowth of songs of war and patriotism, traditionally some of the most bankable staples in country music. Hits such as Toby Keith's ardent flag-waver "The Angry American (Courtesy of the Red, White, and Blue)" and Darryl Worley's rallying "Have You Forgotten?" had enormous unifying power with the record-buying public. But now, with the nation divided in its opinion about whether the United States should have gone to battle in Iraq, Nashville has shifted its focus to put a face on the individual soldier, as in Tracy Lawrence's "If I Don't Make It Back."

"When a war first starts everybody's very behind the effort," explains Tony Lane, the co-writer of John Michael Montgomery's 2004 hit, "Letters From Home," one of the most affecting songs of its type. "But as the conflict goes on and on, people begin to think we have another quagmire, another Vietnam, and the music industry goes along with that. The war is just not as popular and people want it over with, even as they stand behind the soldiers who have to do their jobs."

David Lee, Lane's co-writer who got the idea for "Letters From Home" after watching a shaved-headed soldier and his tearful girlfriend saying goodbye at the airport, has corresponded with soldiers in the field. "They played that song on a Bradley fighting vehicle in Baghdad, and one of the soldiers told me every guy in the Bradley was crying, it just touched them so much," Lee recalls. "But (song) publishers discourage more of these now because they've been done."

Trace Adkins' "Arlington," sung from the point of view of a fallen soldier buried in the famed military cemetery, debuted on the charts in late 2005 and climbed to No. 16 before Adkins himself pulled the plug. Why? Because some of the families of soldiers deployed in active combat zones objected to the lyrics.

And with a sense of uncertainty overall, even songs of loss that aren't inspired by war, such as "Live Like You

Were Dying," Tim McGraw's 2005 megahit about living each day to the fullest, and his more current "My Old Friend," still speak to those who have undergone profound personal struggles as a result of war.

"People write songs about emotion now," explains songwriter Lee. "There's more sentiment about loss and healing, from cancer or any other tragedy. And people talk about God more."

He's right. Diamond Rio's latest single, "God Only Cries," is a new example, while Carrie Underwood's "Jesus, Take the Wheel" hugged the top spot for six weeks. She thinks its success proves that radio listeners were hungry for something to relate to on a spiritual level.

"Many fans tell me that 'Jesus, Take the Wheel' really means something to them," notes Carrie. "I think the most memorable stories are from wives telling me how their husbands cried when they heard it."

Brett James, one of the song's co-writers, has also witnessed strong emotional reaction to the hit. "The chorus is spoken directly to God in a cry out for help and an admission of faith," notes Brett. "It seems to me that trusting and believing that there is someone bigger than ourselves—a higher power—might be the most important thing you can do when faced with tragedy. A friend told me that he had recently attended a funeral for a 16-year-old girl who had died in an auto accident. Her favorite song had been 'Jesus, Take the Wheel' and they placed a CD of it in her casket. I was really struck by that."

Carrie notes that some country singers seemed afraid to express their faith through music in recent years, seeing it as risky. "I think it goes in patterns, and [you're now seeing that] country and gospel have always had a connection with each other, too."

The unexpected success of Alan Jackson's current CD,

Precious Memories—a collection of 15 traditional hymns—is unassailable proof of that. While Jackson recorded it as a Christmas present for his mother, and never meant for it to be released commercially or to lead a trend, the album is the only gospel recording in history to debut at No. 1 on *Billboard's* Top Country Albums chart. Furthermore, the tall Georgian is the first country performer to debut an album of all spiritual material at No. 1 on the Top Christian Albums and Top Christian & Gospel Albums charts.

Alan is, however, only one of several country artists who have devoted entire albums to gospel and religious music in the past year. Others include Charlie Daniels' *Songs From the Longleaf Pines: A Gospel Bluegrass Collection* and Randy Travis' *Glory Train*. Such yearnings bear out what Carrie sees in the near future.

"I think there are lots of singers out there who wanted to do more music like this, but were afraid it would not be accepted. Once a couple of singers do a spiritual song in a way that even nonreligious people can relate to, it makes other artists braver. It's not a secret that so many country listeners come from the Bible Belt. We're just good people who like good music."

Spirituality on the Charts

Steve Wariner's "Holes in the Floor of Heaven" won two CMA awards in 1998.

"Jesus, Take the Wheel" went No. 1 this year for Carrie Underwood.

Vince Gill's "Go Rest High on That Mountain" was the CMA's '96 Song of the Year.

George Strait's "You'll Be There" made it to No. 4 in 2005.

Kenny Chesney soared to No. 2 with "Who You'd Be Today" in 2005.

Brooks & Dunn's 2006 Top 10 "Believe" sent a strong message.

More songs than ever are dealing with God and spirituality, and a look at the country singles charts in the past—and today—proves it.

Does it just *seem* that more songs are showing their spiritual sides these days— or is it a true trend? A comparison of past *Billboard* singles charts confirms it's for real. When *Country Weekly* examined the charts from the last three decades, we discovered that previous years definitely had spirituality-based hits—Merle Haggard's "Jesus, Take a Hold" in 1970, George Strait's "Love Without End, Amen" in 1990 and Alabama's "Angels Among Us" in 1994 are prime examples. But *nothing* in previous years equals the current chart phenomenon of God and country songs.

Aug. 1, 1976—30 Years Ago
Number of spiritually themed songs in the Top 40: 0

Jan. 10, 1981—25 Years Ago
Number of spiritually themed songs in the Top 40: 0

Oct. 18, 1986—20 Years Ago
Once again, no spiritually themed songs entered the Top 40.

Feb. 9, 1991—15 Years Ago
Number of spiritually themed songs in the Top 40: 2

- No. 3 single: "Walk on Faith" by Mike Reid, which actually dealt more with personal relationships, though some interpreted it as a message of spiritual faith.
- No. 11 single: "Unanswered Prayers" by Garth Brooks. A much more overt statement about religion—*Sometimes I thank God for unanswered prayers.*

July 6, 1996—10 Years Ago

Number of spiritually themed songs in the Top 40: 1
- No. 17: "Ten Thousand Angels" by Mindy McCready. A bit of a stretch, though many fans attached a spiritual meaning to the song about delivering a young girl from evil.

Dec. 29, 2001—5 Years Ago

Number of spiritually themed songs in the Top 40: 2
- No. 19: "Blessed" by Martina McBride • No. 20: "Saints & Angels" by Sara Evans

Oct. 19, 2002—4 Years Ago

Number of spiritually themed songs in the Top 40: 1
- No. 12: "The Good Stuff" by Kenny Chesney

May 24, 2003—3 Years Ago

Number of spiritually themed songs in the Top 40: 3
- No. 1: "Three Wooden Crosses" by Randy Travis
- No. 4: "I Believe" by Diamond Rio
- No. 20: "Concrete Angel" by Martina McBride

"Three Wooden Crosses" was also a hit in the contemporary Christian market, making this an unusual crossover success. The song was significant in kicking off the trend toward spirituality's return to country music.

Feb. 14, 2004—2 Years Ago

Number of spiritually themed songs in the Top 40: 1
- No. 13: "Long Black Train" by Josh Turner

This was the peak position for Josh's debut single, which dealt with sin, forgiveness and ultimate redemption. "Long Black Train" was also played on Christian radio stations in several markets.

March 26, 2005—1+ Years Ago

Number of spiritually themed songs in the Top 40: 4
- No. 1: "That's What I Love About Sunday" by Craig Morgan
- No. 13: "If Heaven" by Andy Griggs
- No. 16: "Drugs or Jesus" by Tim McGraw
- No. 18: "God's Will" by Martina McBride

By hitting the top, "That's What I Love About Sunday," which depicted a typical Sunday morning church service in the South, reinforced the trend toward spirituality in country music. It proved that this theme could resonate with listeners in a huge and significant way.

Dec. 24, 2005—6 Months Ago

Number of spiritually themed songs in the Top 40: 4
- No. 2: "Who You'd Be Today" by Kenny Chesney
- No. 8: "Jesus, Take the Wheel" by Carrie Underwood
- No. 18: "When I Get Where I'm Going" by Brad Paisley, featuring Dolly Parton
- No. 21: "Believe" by Brooks & Dunn

On Dec. 24, there were four spiritually tinted songs in the Top 40, but during 2005, 10 such songs reached the Top 40 of the *Billboard* Hot Country Songs chart. Those hits were Alan Jackson's "Monday Morning Church," "That's

What I Love About Sunday," "Drugs or Jesus," "God's Will," George Strait's "You'll Be There," "If Heaven," "Who You'd Be Today," "Jesus, Take the Wheel," "When I Get Where I'm Going" and "Believe."

Jan. 21–May 20—2006

So far in 2006, the number of spiritually themed songs in the Top 40: 3

On Jan. 21 the spirituality song trend continued, when Carrie Underwood's "Jesus, Take the Wheel" reached the top of the charts, marking the first week of an amazing six weeks at No. 1 for this touching song. On March 4, Brad Paisley's "When I Get Where I'm Going," featuring Dolly Parton, made it to No. 1, and a little over a month later, April 29, Brooks & Dunn's powerful "Believe" peaked at No. 8. By May 20, Diamond Rio's powerful "God Only Cries" was poised to enter *Billboard's* Top 40.

Alanna Nash

Bobby Bare: The Return of the Quiet Outlaw

By Rick Kelly
From *CMA Close Up*

In recent years, there has been growing interest in the iconoclastic group of 1970s Country artists who were loosely collected under the banner of the Outlaw Movement. Current artists release songs that name-check the great artists of that era including Big & Rich's "Rollin'," CMA Female Vocalist of the Year Gretchen Wilson's "Redneck Woman" and Gary Allan's "What Would Willie Do."

CMA Horizon Award winner Dierks Bentley has adopted the rolling, phase-shifted Fender Telecaster sound of Waylon Jennings on hits such as "Lot of Leavin' Left to Do," and Waylon Jennings' son Shooter Jennings has donned the mantle of the outlaw. All of these artists were instrumental in moving Country Music to a new and more contemporary place, and should be remembered and honored. Among them is Bobby Bare.

Born in Ironton, Ohio, in 1935, Bare had a difficult early life. After the death of his mother when he was 5 years old, Bare's family split up and he found work as a teenager on farms, in factories and as an ice-cream vendor. Bare built his first guitar, and at 11 taught himself to play. By his late teens, he was playing with a local band throughout Ohio. In the late 1950s, Bare moved to Los Angeles where he had his first taste of chart success with the talking blues "All American Boy" in 1958, recorded under the name Bill Parsons. The single was a Top 5 country and pop single in the United States, and approached the Top 20 in the United Kingdom. After a stint in the Army, Bare returned to his singing and songwriting career, achieving some minor success in the pop music world.

In the early 1960s, Bare, encouraged by friend and legendary songwriter Harlan Howard, moved to Nashville and was signed by Chet Atkins to RCA Records. He became the first major label artist in Nashville to produce his own albums and quickly found success with his first single "Shame On Me" breaking into the Top 20 on the Country charts and peaking at No. 23 on the pop charts. His follow-up single, "Detroit City" was a crossover hit which peaked inside the Top 5 on the country and pop charts, and was awarded the 1963 Grammy for Best Country Performance. This was the beginning of a run of eleven Top 10 singles and more than thirty Top 20 singles between 1962 and 1981.

Unlike many of his contemporaries, Bare was not content to hand the creative reins to record producers and pick only songs written in Nashville. Endowed with a great musical curiosity and a love of truly great songwriting from the entire spectrum of music, Bare began to record songs by gifted writers from different genres. He recorded songs from rock and folk luminaries including J.J. Cale, Gene Clark, the Rolling Stones and Ian Tyson. The legendary rock promoter Bill Graham called Bare the "Springsteen of country" and signed on as his manager in the mid-1970s.

Bare was also masterful in recognizing great new songwriting talents. He was among the first country artists to record songs by the new breed of songwriters who were blurring the lines between country and folk. The writers that Bare championed included such now legendary names as Guy Clark, Rodney Crowell and Billy Joe Shaver.

Perhaps the most significant songwriter/singer partnership that Bare entered into was with Shel Silverstein. In 1973, Bare released *Lullabys, Legends and Lies*, a double-album of Silverstein compositions.

The concept album became Bare's most successful release, peaking at No. 5. It also yielded the most successful singles of Bare's career, the No. 1 "Marie Laveau" and the No. 2 "Daddy, What If," a vocal duet with Bare's 6-year-old son Bobby Jr. Eventually, Bare would release three albums consisting mostly or entirely of Silverstein's songs.

By the mid-1980s, Bare's album sales had dropped off, and he was no longer getting the radio airplay he'd enjoyed earlier in his career. After a meeting with his label in which he was asked to "do some Bob Seger," Bare asked to be released from his record deal.

"There was no real reason to do albums anymore because there was nowhere to go with them," Bare said. "They basically told me 'Come back when you're younger.'"

Bare harbors no resentment about this turn of events.

"The music business is, and always has been about young people," he said. "When they were playing my records, I was glad they were playing them. But that meant they weren't playing Hank Snow or Roy Acuff or Lefty Frizzell. Eventually they started playing newer artists and stopped playing me."

Bare continues to work on the road, playing "more dates than I'd really like to" in venues throughout the country.

In November 2005, after a 22-year hiatus from recording as a solo artist, Bare released *The Moon Was Blue* on Dualtone Records, featuring the single and video "Are You Sincere."

Critics have embraced the album: "The album combines an indie-rock sensibility with Nashville sound arrangement, making the elder Bare the likely candidate to become country's legend du jour." — *USA Today*; "... the work of a crafty master." — *Entertainment Weekly*; and "Astonishing ... Nothing short of a masterpiece." — *L.A. Weekly*.

The Moon Was Blue is a collection of classic songs, and features the mature, burnished vocals of Bare Sr., over the airy and playful co-production of his son, Bare Jr., and Mark Nevers.

"I know that people my age and younger have no idea what my dad does," Bare Jr. said. "I wanted to get to the more soulful kind of stuff that he did in the '60s. That's why we picked the songs that we did. The most difficult part of the project was getting dad out of the bass boat long enough to come to the studio to make the record."

Bare Sr. said his son was instrumental in the creation of the new album.

"Bobby kept pressuring me to come in and do some recording with him, and after he'd brought it up a number of times, I realized it was something important to him," Bare Sr. said. "I told him that I was just going to be the singer, and that he and Mark could do whatever they wanted with the record."

The eclectic production of the album serves the songs and the voice of Bare Sr. well on songs including "All in the Game," "Everybody's Talking at Me," "Yesterday When I Was Young" and "The Ballad of Lucy Jordan." The latter is a final nod to Silverstein, who died in 1999.

Asked about plans for future albums, Bare Sr. answered with a joke. "Well, I haven't planned to do one, but after you turn 70, you don't look that far ahead," he said. "I would like to do another record, though."

There is wisdom to be gained from someone with a half-century of recording and touring experience. Asked for his advice for young artists to ensure longevity, Bare Sr. replied, "Write and record great songs. Lots of people can sing, but not just anybody can write a great song."

Rick Kelly

DEL McCOURY: LEADING MAN

By Chris Stuart
From *Bluegrass Unlimited*

On a rural road in Hendersonville, Tenn., as houses become farther apart, past weathered barns sits a five-acre parcel of land and a comfortable, well-maintained home belonging to Del and Jean McCoury. You can hear birdsong and the rustle of deer crossing the property. It's so calm that if you didn't know better, you'd assume this was the home of some retired musician (Hendersonville is just a few minutes from Nashville), the children long gone, and only the weight of a tour bus parked to the side, serving as a reminder of a busier time.

But the truth is far different. There probably has never been a busier time for Del McCoury and his family. As the 67-year-old patriarch, Del oversees a thriving band and business, built on a solid foundation of talent and hard work. He's earned every bit of his success, but he wears that success lightly, with humility, humor, and sincere appreciation.

As a second generation bluegrass artist, Del is a link between the old-style bossman bandleader and a modern owner of a music corporation. He's very much a leader, and very aware of his music, who he is, and what he wants his legacy to be.

What makes Del different from the old stereotypical bluegrass bossman is that he's a leader by example. He surrounds himself with people he can trust, letting them do what they do best. But his integrity, musical and personal, guides those people. As he says, "If you let them do what they're good at, then it's better for everybody." No bandleader has a more devoted team or a more devout fan base. It all emanates from a man who has followed the golden rule for nearly fifty years in a business where gold is the rule.

Del's wife, Jean, a sparkling detail-oriented dynamo, is a full partner in every sense of the word: in marriage, family, and business. She guides the daily spending decisions of McCoury Music (the record label and publishing company). She also travels with Del, Ronnie, and Rob, taking care of CD and merchandise sales. And she keeps track of all the birthdays and events of an ever increasing brood of grandchildren. Del says, "I don't know what I'd do without her."

Stan Strickland and Chris Harris of Rainmaker Management, based in Tampa, Fla., manage both the Del McCoury Band and the daily operations of the record label and publishing entity. Bobby Cudd of Monterey Artists handles the booking of the band, and Ken Weinstein of Big Hassle Media is in charge of publicity. The network of people extends out to include more family, friends, employees, and street teams of fans.

A bandleader can't go it alone. The good ones not only know how to build a band and maintain it, but also know how to build a support system of business associates that can take their music to the most people while bringing in the most money. And only the very best can still maintain a sense of themselves and their music. Del is one of the few in any musical genre who does that. He doesn't concern himself with petty jealousies, regrets, or transient ambitions. He'll take his time in making a decision, making sure he has all the facts, talking to the right people; but once he makes a decision, it's made and he moves on. Jean explains,

"He'll ask for opinions from people that he respects and he knows care about him, but he'll make the final decision, and once he's made it, there's no changing his mind." He's open to new ideas, but not at the expense of changing the music to the degree that it no longer is his. He trusts in the ability of his music, his voice, and his sound to carry new songs to new audiences.

He claims none of this, of course. It's not his style to talk about himself. When he does talk about the success of the Del McCoury Band and McCoury Music, Del's quick to credit everyone around him. And the stories he tells of the past are mostly about funny incidents and people who mean a lot to him, about good times and hard times. But his ideas about leadership come out. "When I'm singing, that's when I'm depending on my band behind me, and their timing, their rhythm. So, they all have to be leaders in a way."

Tim O'Brien, who's had Del sing on several of his recordings, says, "I guess he doesn't tell people what to play, but praises them when they play how and what he likes. I know he showed his sons some things on their instruments, and they know that he knows how it should be. It's so nice that they want to play his music and pay respect to it."

Both Ronnie and Rob McCoury talk about how their Dad never insisted that they learn to play bluegrass. He encouraged them simply by showing them how to do it, and showing them how good it can be when a band is all working together. As Rob said, "Our whole sound is based around that rhythm guitar. He's really good at getting the best out of you without telling you."

He also lets the band, especially Ronnie, have a large say in recording, arranging, and selection of material. Ronnie learned a lot from Jerry Douglas when Jerry produced the band in the '90s. But it is Del's sound and Del's voice that ultimately guides those decisions. "We all have a hand in arranging, but Dad knows what suits him and how to sing it," Ronnie says. It's that trust he places in others that has made Del McCoury a success. It's also meant that sometimes people have taken advantage of him, his faith in human nature sometimes outrunning his knowledge of human faults. But he carries no grudges. He's someone who early-on decided that the weight of those grudges is not worth the effort.

Bluegrass fans love to gossip and the Del McCoury Band has had its share of rumors spread about them in recent years about events such as the band's playing for more jamgrass audiences, Del's strained relationship with Steve Earle on their combined tour, the possibility of Del's retirement, and most recently and painfully, the departure of long-time bass player Mike Bub.

While these are all important events and concerns, they are also typical of things that a bandleader has to deal with on a daily basis: growing a fan base, protection of artistic rights, maintaining artistic and personal integrity, knowing how to prepare for a future after music, and making tough decisions about bandmembers. Del has made these decisions over the course of a long career. "I know I've made some bad decisions, too, along the way, but in the very end I make the decisions."

One very good decision was to expand the band's audience by acting on its growing reputation among the fans of jamgrass bands such as Phish and Leftover Salmon. While some artists in their sixties might have rested on a well-worn festival circuit and balked at the possibility of losing their old fans, Del was able to take this chance because he knew that he was staying true to his sound. The jamgrass fans were coming to his music. "I was always that way about taking chances, you know. I never was afraid to really take a chance." It has meant a dramatic increase in both sales and

Del McCoury: Leading Man

visibility for both Del and bluegrass music among a younger crowd.

The Steve Earle/Del McCoury Band collaboration started out as mutual admiration (Del had recorded one of Steve's songs), and the release of *The Mountain* in 1999 was a powerful combination of edgy yet traditional-styled songwriting with the locomotive precision of the Del McCoury Band, one of the best albums of that year. A tour was set up, but it quickly became apparent that some of Steve Earle's use of profanity on stage did not appeal to Del. "I thought, 'What did I get into?' because he was using foul language on stage and I just never had that in a show of mine and I thought, 'Some of my bluegrass people are going to come to these shows.'"

As the relationship deteriorated, Del felt that his own band was not being respected on a basic level. So, Del ended the musical relationship, quickly and effectively. Eventually, the tour was completed, but it was one instance of Del trying something new, but not willing to change so much that he would lose integrity for himself, his family, band, and fans.

The Mike Bub situation is more complicated and more painful for all involved, but there have been several times in Del's career where he's felt the need for change. "I just felt in my mind, for the music, I just needed to make a change. Mike's a great bass player, and he can play with anybody in town. I really wish him well. I like Mike."

And rumors of Del's retirement have been floating around for years. When asked about it, Del responded directly, "I'm really not thinking about retiring or coming off the road because I still like the road and it's so much easier now. I used to drive my own bus. I'm in pretty good financial shape, but I still like to play music and entertain folks." Stan Strickland also confirms that Del has no plans to retire, but that possibly he'll cut back to around sixty shows a year over the next few years.

Del would like to see his sons go out and play on their own, too, something Ronnie and Rob have done to a limited extent in recent years, but both have been committed to the Del McCoury Band for so long that it's not something that's a high priority with them right now.

All of these concerns and issues are connected. Del McCoury is a bandleader who does make the decisions and who guides the direction of his family, band, and business. He does it in a quieter way than a Bill Monroe or a Jimmy Martin, but it's an effective way that has reaped tremendous rewards over the years. Del certainly doesn't micro manage and he doesn't lead by intimidation. It's hard to even imagine that. He leads by showing the way. "You have to surround yourself with good people and I've been fortunate."

Del is possibly the most admired and most liked person in bluegrass and country music. He commands a quiet respect, love, and admiration from almost everyone. But he also remains true to his vision of his music, to himself and his family, and to those business associates around him. As Jean said, "He demands as much of himself musically as he does of those around him. Also, he understands that fans are spending their hard-earned money to see the band's shows, so he makes sure to always show his appreciation and respect for the fans and tries to keep the music fresh every night. That's why he never uses a set list and always takes requests."

If any of us men could look like anyone, it would be Del. He combines the authority of a graying air-force general with a Steve Martin boyish grin. He's trim and fit, although he'll pat his stomach and joke that he needs to cut back some. The lines in his face are well-balanced between those of worry and laughter. He's been no stranger to work, having spent many years working on a farm, at a steel plant, and in a sawmill, but it's not bent him down. He stands tall.

Born Delano Floyd McCoury in Bakersville, N.C., on February 1, 1939, during the Franklin Delano Roosevelt administration, Del's family soon re-located to a dairy farm in York County, Pa. He grew up singing in church, working the farm, and learning music from his older brother G.C. McCoury, who introduced Del to the sound of bluegrass by listening to 78s and also tuning in to the Grand Ole Opry on the radio. "I learned to play guitar first from G.C., and then I heard Earl Scruggs and said, "Man, that's what I want to do!' That's about 1950."

Del eventually landed a gig as banjo player with his first mentor as a bandleader, Keith Daniels, a mandolin player who owned a restaurant in Hanover, Pa. "He was a great musician and singer. I'd say that was my early learning as far as managing a band. I later worked for Jack Cooke, but, at the time, we didn't play out much. He had just quit Bill Monroe. I was one of the first musicians that he had and we just played this little club called the Chapel Café in downtown Baltimore. We'd play there three nights a week and he didn't book out much. The next guy I worked for was Bill Monroe and I learned about the road then."

Del's first concert with Monroe was as a banjo player and baritone singer at New York University in February 1963. Monroe traveled north and picked up Jack Cooke and Del along the way. "We didn't rehearse anything, we just walked right on stage. That's the Monroe way. There were a lot of people there who later became great musicians, Pete Wernick, Tony Trischka. I think Grisman was in the audience that night."

Once back in Nashville, Monroe extended an offer to Del to audition for a regular spot as a Blue Grass Boy. Del wasn't that interested in heading down to Nashville because he enjoyed playing so much with Jack Cooke in Baltimore, but his friend Bobby Diamond told him, "Some people would kill for that job," and told Del that he'd drive him down there in his Cadillac if he'd audition.

Del assumed Monroe wanted a banjo player, so he showed up at the Clarkson Hotel on Eighth Avenue in Nashville, as Monroe had requested, for the audition. But another banjo player had also come to town to audition for Monroe's Bill Keith, who would become the seminal melodic-style player with Monroe. Monroe took them to the National Life and Accident Insurance building, where the Friday Night Opry originated, and he asked Del to audition on guitar. Del's not even sure how Monroe knew he played guitar. Monroe told them that he'd try them out for two weeks. Both of them got the job.

Bill Monroe was the original bluegrass bossman: tough, arrogant to a fault, protective, highly-driven, and successful. "It was kind of a shock to me in a way, you know. He was the type of guy, he would never tell you anything. He wouldn't tell you, 'Now sing this note' or how to play, but it seemed that fiddle players' I think that fiddle was like a voice he'd work with them."

But Del did learn about life on the road, about good rhythm in a band, and about singing. "I realized how important singing was in a band. Monroe always sang to his lead singers. But I was singing to him, either consciously or unconsciously. I had a real good ear. I knew when he said, 'You won't know when I go from my natural voice to falsetto', but I would know, so I would go to a falsetto voice. I could hear that tone change and I'd just do that to match him. I learned a lot of singing."

He did one recording session with Monroe, on January 28, 1964, where he recorded "Roll On Buddy, Roll On," "Legend Of The Blue Ridge Mountains," and "One Of

God's Sheep." In February of 1964, Del left the band with fiddler Billy Baker and headed to California. They had been offered jobs in a band called the Golden State Boys fronted by Hal Poindexter. Del and Jean married and went out west together. That band turned out to have a regular gig with Cal Worthington Dodge in Los Angeles, but didn't travel enough for Del to make the kind of money he needed, and with Jean being homesick, they headed back to York County, Pa., in the fall of 1964.

Del was 25 years old, newly married, back to work, and just wanting to play music. "I loved to play music, and I'm not sure I even thought about leading a band. So, I started playing these little places on my own. Just calling up guys that I knew to play. And still, I got to thinking, I'm going to have to do the emceeing because these guys they won't say nothing, and I got to do all the singing because they can't sing good, and I got to do all the rhythm playing, you know, so that's when I started thinking, if I'm doing all this, I might as well get my own band."

It was Bobby Diamond, again, who came up with the name for the Dixie Pals. One night while playing a club in Baltimore, one of the patrons asked the band what their name was and Diamond shouted out, "The Dixie Pals." Del turned around and said, "It is?" Diamond had gotten the name from another band that had just broken up. The name stuck, and it would be Del McCoury and the Dixie Pals off and on until his sons joined the band. First Ronnie joined on mandolin and then Rob on banjo, becoming the Del McCoury Band in the late 1980s.

The twenty years of playing from 1967 to 1987 were highlighted by some great bands and recordings with Paul Silvius on banjo, John Glik on fiddle, his brother Jerry [McCoury] on bass, and many other artists who contributed to the McCoury sound. Del was also writing songs such as

"Dreams" and "Rain, Please Go Away" and appearing at bluegrass festivals, traveling whenever he could get away from work.

These were years when Del had a young family and was working a day job as well. "I worked pretty hard. Seemed like every job I had, I worked hard. I thought, well, if you're going to do it, you might as well do it right. And it was hard for me to be working and playing too, but back then I could go without sleep. I was fortunate to get a job with my wife's uncle. He needed someone to help him in the woods to cut timber and he was going to pay me good. Grover Gardner, the one I wrote that "Loggin' Man" song about. He knew me well enough and said, 'When you need to take off and play music, you just tell me, and go ahead.'"

Another major influence on Del as a bandleader was Don Reno. Del and Jerry played with Don briefly in 1969. Del saw a master entertainer, musician, songwriter, and someone who treated people fairly and openly. "That guy was so talented at so many things. He was a great bandleader and emcee. And the greatest songwriter I was ever around was Don Reno."

Between 1968 and 1988, Del put out seven albums on various labels: Arhoolie, Grassound, Rebel, Rounder, Revonah, and a "Live In Japan" album released by Copper Creek. He was also learning about being a bandleader. Occasionally, he'd have to make a change in the band. "It was hard for me to do, because I like people, and I realize that everybody has faults and I have my faults. But then I realized, well, if there's someone making the band sound bad or running the name down, then I had to get rid of them. Most of the time, nobody ever would quit, so I'd have to fire them. And it's a tough thing to do."

Returning to Rounder Records in 1988, Del recorded "Don't Stop The Music" with Ronnie, Rob, and Jerry. In

1992, the family moved to Nashville. Del added Mike Bub on bass and Jason Carter on fiddle, and for the next 15 years, the band toured and recorded together, winning an unprecedented nine International Bluegrass Music Association Entertainer Of The Year awards, along with Del's four Male Vocalist Of The Year awards.

Three subsequent albums on Rounder, *Blue Side Of Town* (1992), *Deeper Shade Of Blue* (1993), and *Cold Hard Facts* (1996), established the McCoury family sound, and Del himself, as the most widely heard voices in bluegrass. It was a good example of working for forty years to be an overnight success.

In 1999 with his contract with Rounder Records completed, Del decided to go with Skaggs Family Records. They released two successful albums, *Family* (1999) and *Del & The Boys* (2001). Part of coming to Skaggs Family Records included working with a new manager, Stan Strickland (a preacher's son from north Florida), who had worked for major labels for most of his career. Stan began working with Del to regain artistic and commercial control over his songs, recordings, and merchandise, something that most artists, unless they retain control from the beginning, can only dream about doing. "I saw a guy who had worked his tail off, and everybody around him had made money, but Del hadn't," Strickland said, "I consider myself very fortunate to be able to work with Del and call him a friend. I have met very few people in my life that I respect as much, and not one that I have greater respect for."

Part of regaining control of Del's artistic value was the decision in 2002 to start a new record label, McCoury Music. The idea originally came from Ronnie. At first, Del, Jean, and Stan were not that interested in building the infrastructure necessary to run a label. With Del's success, though, and with bluegrass at it's hottest after Nashville began to wake up to the phenomenon of *O Brother, Where Art Thou?*, Del was approached by numerous record labels including that of T-Bone Burnett, who once called the Del McCoury Band "the greatest rock-and-roll band I have ever heard." Ultimately, after weighing several very lucrative offers, Del and his family decided to start their own label (deciding they knew best how to market their own sound), and by retaining control of their recordings, they could best prepare for the future and hopefully reap the rewards of a lifetime's work.

It was an economic decision, but also a personal one for Del, because he knew that by owning and controlling the masters of his recordings as well as the direction of his life and legacy, he could best represent himself, his family, and his music. And he could show other artists that there was another way of doing things to benefit themselves. As his manager Strickland said, "If I could guarantee Del McCoury a platinum record by changing his sound, I wouldn't even have that conversation with him. He's never been driven by anything except the music and his relationship with his fans. This is a man who cannot be bought."

The first release on McCoury Music's *It's Just The Night* (2003) was highly successful and the record label was in the black after nine months, something unheard of for an independent label. And on October 25, 2003, Del became a member of the Grand Ole Opry, completing a circle that began with him first listening to bluegrass on the very same show when he was a boy.

The second release on McCoury Music, *The Company We Keep* (2005) won Del and the band their first Grammy (after six nominations) for Best Bluegrass Album Of The Year.

The newest release is perhaps Del's best and most important release to date, an all-gospel album called *The*

Promised Land. Del started on a gospel album many years ago with Rounder, but band changes prevented him from completing it. So, after nearly fifty years in bluegrass and including gospel music as a part of almost each show, Del McCoury is finally releasing a gospel album. "It's hard to get an independent label to get behind a gospel album. It's a little different market. But when I got my own label, I started thinking, now I'm going to do my gospel album." Ronnie says this album is one of his father's "proudest moments." But in typical Del fashion, it's not just a re-hash of old favorites. The album is historic in the release of seven previously unrecorded songs by the great songwriter Albert Brumley. Ronnie was approached by Albert's son, Jackson Brumley, with a demo of songs and as Del began listening, he heard gems that suited his voice and style.

Other songs include great new originals by Shawn Camp, Ronnie Bowman, Bill Walker, Billy and Terry Smith, and a song co-written by Del and Jerry Salley titled "Ain't Nothin' Going to Come Up Today Me and the Good Lord Can't Handle," which comes from words on Roy Acuff's dressing room door at the Grand Ole Opry. Of special note is Billy Walker's "Gold Under My Feet," a seemingly lost Flatt & Scruggs classic that features Del and Ronnie's voices sounding more like brothers than father and son. Rob complements the album with his excellent banjo skills, along with Jason Carter on fiddle and newest member Alan Bartram on bass.

It's fitting that Del should be putting out a gospel album now, because the one overriding feeling you get from sitting down and talking with him is that he's someone who is grateful and humbled by his and his family's success. His voice is as powerful, supple, and nuanced as it was forty years ago. More importantly though, it's the voice of a man who practices what he preaches, who can carry the weight of a moral message and deliver it, and who can still lead by example.

Faith Hill Never Stopped Being a 'Mississippi Girl'

By Michael McCall
From *CMA Close Up*

Faith Hill peppers her conversation with sudden bursts of uninhibited laughter and with phrases like "Bless your heart," "Oh my gosh," "God bless them," "Isn't that sweet?" and "Don't you just love her?"

In other words, she sounds exactly like thousands of other 30-something women raised in religious families in small Southern towns. Like many others, she moved to the city, worked hard, found success and gave shape to her dreams. Yet she held onto a piece of her rural identity, not only in the way she talks, but in the way she lives. As the song says, "a Mississippi girl don't change her ways just 'cause everybody knows her name."

Only now, after Hurricane Katrina, taking pride in being a Mississippi native has assumed new layers of meaning. As with many things creative, Hill's artistic move has, by coincidence, taken on significance she never could have predicted.

"I'm so glad I am out there telling the world I'm from Mississippi right now," Hill said. "It's something I've always been proud of, but with all the devastation and damage, there's a lot of concern and I'm feeling a lot of connection."

For Hill, Mississippi's plight resembles experiencing a loved one facing a serious illness. Suddenly she wants to visit more often, and home occupies a larger part of her thoughts and her heart.

"I have so many friends and relatives along the coast," she explained. "They're doing OK, but you worry about them more. My parents and my older brother live north of the coast, and they were without power or water for about a week and a half or two weeks. There were a lot of trees down in Star, but it's nothing like on the coast."

Hill has toured the damaged areas along the Gulf Coast, and as with other eyewitnesses, she says that television footage and print photos can't convey the vastness of the damage. "I couldn't believe it when I went there to see it," she explained. "It's just mind-blowing, the devastation. I'd spent a lot of time there in the past, and I'd just recently been to Biloxi to work before all this happened. The amount of destruction is just unbelievable. It was so widespread and so far inland."

The storms and floods came as the single, "Mississippi Girl," from Hill's album *Fireflies* gained daily radio play and sat at the top of the charts. What surprised Hill was how she had to defend her choice to record a song about her raising and defend putting it on an album that had a more stripped-down, acoustic sound than her two previous albums, 2002's *Cry* and 1999's *Breathe*.

"There's been so much said about it, and a lot of it is just plain wrong," she said. "But how do you defend it? Oh my gosh, I've even had the question, 'Is your hair dark now because you're going back to your roots?'"

She lets out one of her characteristic bursts of laughter. "I mean, what do you say to that? Is that supposed to be a joke?"

She continues to laugh, but it dies down to a somber chuckle as she shakes her head in disbelief. "You know, to me, I've never left my roots behind," she continued. "I didn't on *Cry*, and I didn't on *Breathe*. They just sound differently because at that time, I was interested in going into a different part of who I am and what I want to sing. I cut my musical teeth in the church, in raise-the-roof Pentecostal churches. Of course, I was raised on country music as well, on Tammy Wynette and Loretta Lynn and George and Dolly and Reba.

"But those are two different things — the church music and the country music. So my musical tastes are so extreme. I feel like I'm influenced by all the music I grew up with, and all the music that I love listening to now. Trying to find my place in all that is sometimes very complicated."

She accepts that her decisions can be confusing to others. "I know that *Cry* wasn't something that worked for country radio, but it sold 3 million copies, and no one ever talks about that," she said with a laugh. "It's written about like it was a bomb, but it wasn't. I'm still very proud of it."

What she can't accept, she says, is people describing *Fireflies* as a calculated move — a return to straightforward country music inspired only by business, not artistic merit.

"That doesn't even fit into my realm of reality," she said. "I couldn't be less like that. The toughest part of all this is hearing that kind of criticism. That's what hurts. People mistake your actions for ... whatever. When someone can't see that things are honest and come from your heart, that's difficult to take. But I'm a big girl. You just have to stand tall and walk forward."

Hill says she created *Fireflies* because songs that came along that inspired her worked best in a sparer, rootsier setting. And after a couple of albums in which her music grew increasingly fuller and more theatrical, she felt a desire to do something simpler and more straightforward.

John Rich of Big & Rich and Adam Shoenfeld co-wrote "Mississippi Girl" for Hill. "I basically stalked Faith Hill because I wanted to write a song for her," said Rich, who got to know the singer during Big & Rich's first national tour as opening act for Tim McGraw. Hill and the couple's daughters often joined McGraw during the tour, with Hill dressing down in her ballcap, jeans, T-shirts and sneakers. Rich got to see a side of the superstar few ever do, and she impressed him with how down-to-earth she was.

"I've always admired the emotional way she sings," Rich said. "I knew I wanted to write a song for her. But I started hiding out watching her, and I wanted to capture that part of her in a song."

She had already gathered some other key songs including "I Ain't Gonna Take It Anymore" and the album's second hit, "Like We Never Loved at All." She'd put aside a jazzy tune called "Paris" (a hidden track on *Fireflies*), at first thinking it might be too unusual for her to record. But as the album filled out, she realized it wasn't so different after all.

Then, as she thought she was nearing the end of recording, Nashville song publisher Melanie Howard sent Hill a song by Lori McKenna, a Massachusetts singer-songwriter and mother of five. Hill listened to the song, "If You Ask," and flipped for it. She immediately requested to hear everything McKenna had written. It turned out to be quite a lot — McKenna had released four independent albums.

"I couldn't believe the honesty in her writing," Hill said. "It was so human. I just fell in love with her. There was a while there that I didn't listen to anything but her records. I knew I was going to cut several of her songs."

Besides "If You Ask," Hill cut McKenna's "Stealing Kisses" and "Fireflies," which became the album's title. The two appeared together on an *Oprah* segment devoted to Hill. McKenna has since been signed to Warner Bros. Records and had her most recent album, *Bittertown*, re-

released by the major label.

"There's still not a week that goes by that I don't listen to Lori's music," Hill said. "She just kills me. And I love her as a person now. I've really gotten to know her and she's just a great girl — very funny, very smart and a great mom."

At one point, Hill thought McKenna's "Stealing Kisses" would be the leadoff cut. But others convinced her to start with "Mississippi Girl," a decision that obviously worked well.

"It was a good way to introduce myself back into the market," she conceded. "It was what I needed to say at that moment, and it's fun to sing live and the crowd loves it. If it was up to me, I could've done a whole album of Lori McKenna songs, but it's good to hit different marks on an album. You have to have those feel-good songs that make you feel great."

So there she goes again — defending herself for having contradictory creative impulses. She laughs loud and long at that thought. "You know, I have to walk to the beat of my own drum, for sure," she sighed. "Who wants to be predictable, to be a follower? I have three daughters, and I want them to see that I follow my heart and don't always take the safe, easy way. I'd want them to be the same way."

Michael McCall

Brad Paisley Moves up from Corn dogs to Catered Meals

Country crooner trades the Ferris wheel for arena shows and ACM acclaim

By Peter Cooper
From The Tennessean

ST. LOUIS, MO — On a late March afternoon, St. Louis' hockey arena was starting to look less like a sporting venue and more like... well, like a mess, but that was only temporary.

More than 50 workers scrambled around, already six hours into a work day that began at 7 a.m. They were hoisting equipment, laying cables and preparing what would eventually be a major country music concert headlined by Brad Paisley.

At 1 p.m., sound was achieved as Tom T. Hall's "Country Is" pumped through the finally raised speakers. These days, country is a big ol' business. Meanwhile, Paisley was waking up on his tour bus, which was parked inside the arena, near two Zamboni machines.

The main floor at the Savvis Center was a world of levers, pulleys, chains and girders, and the ruler of that world was production coordinator Kevin Freeman. "Every day out here we build a little city and hang it from the ceiling," Freeman said.

That little city is growing, as Paisley — who leads the Academy of Country Music awards field going into Tuesday evening's show with six nominations — is now among country's A-listers in terms of touring power, according to *Billboard* magazine's senior touring editor, Ray Waddell.

That's a contrast to Paisley's early touring days, when he played on flatbed trucks, endured dust storms onstage and scoured for county fair food. "I wouldn't trade any of those experiences," he said upon rising at 1:30 p.m. "Now we get good catering, these nice arenas . . . you don't take it for granted that you're not eating corn dogs anymore."

Most country artists, even many of the ones who score big radio hits, perform on what is known as the "soft ticket" market, meaning venues such as casinos and fairs, where crowds will gather regardless of the act and where performers can make decent guaranteed money without having to count on people paying for a ticket that allows entrance into a concert and nothing else. Someone who pays $60 to see a concert at a stadium, amphitheatre or arena has purchased a "hard ticket."

"A few years ago, we tried a tour or two on the hard ticket market and it didn't work," Paisley said. "We didn't lose money, but didn't make money either, and it didn't feel right. I just wasn't there yet; we needed more hits. I told management, 'If there's not a poker table or a Ferris wheel there, I'm not playing it for a while.' "

Having scored hits "Alcohol," "Celebrity," "Mud on the Tires," "When I Get Where I'm Going" and "Whiskey Lullaby" in the past three years, Paisley has adjusted that philosophy.

Brad Paisley Moves up from Corn Dogs to Catered Meals

"It's like knocking at a door and finally, all of a sudden, it opens," said Brad Garrett, who runs Polo Productions and who promoted the show at Savvis Center. "A couple of years ago, it finally just blew up for Brad."

There was no Ferris wheel for Paisley's St. Louis show, though there was a poker table. Along with the amps and instruments and gear, Paisley's tour buses haul a poker table where he and his bandmates gather to wind down after the concert. Paisley's tour day itineraries are mapped out long before he makes it to a city. For the St. Louis gig, he left Nashville on a bus at 4 a.m., arrived in St. Louis in the morning and rested on the bus while the crew built the set. He woke in time to go to a dining room and eat the catered lunch (which ends at 2 p.m., big star or not) and prepare for the sound check at 3 p.m.

Printouts posted on the backstage walls tell everyone the time for dinner (5 p.m.), the time for sound checks for Paisley (3 p.m.) and opening act Sara Evans (4 p.m.), the time the arena doors open (7 p.m.), the time between sets (15 minutes) and the time Paisley will spend onstage (75 minutes). The printouts also report the time the buses roll out for the next night's gig in Cedar Falls, Iowa (2 a.m.), the total miles to Cedar Falls (408) and the anticipated arrival time (8:50 a.m.).

Paisley enjoys the relative comforts of the places he's playing these days but tends to fret as much as he did back when it was small clubs, fairs and festivals.

"When you're as new at this as I am, doing it on this scale, it's on my mind all the time to make sure people walk away feeling like they got their money's worth," he said. "It's a completely different scale. It's like if you played touch football in your back yard, then went to Lambeau Field and played touch football. You go, 'OK, we're actually going to have to go 100 yards to score a touchdown,' and thats harder."

To cover that distance, Paisley uses extensive video to augment and accent his songs. A cartoon he drew is shown on the large video screen during his "Time Warp" instrumental, while the performance of "Alcohol" features footage from local bars: The video crew scouts out each city's watering holes before the show. And Grand Ole Opry great Little Jimmy Dickens and actor William Shatner also make appearances on the big screen.

"In the beginning, I would talk a lot and tell stories and jokes and goof around, but that doesn't work in these venues," Paisley said, sitting at lunch in his black Nike shirt and baseball cap. "I enjoyed that part of learning to entertain, but I also enjoy replacing that with Shatner coming up on the screen and introducing 'Celebrity.' It's a different way of entertaining."

Promoter Garrett put it this way: "People don't come to hear a show. They come to see one. They come already understanding what the writer or the singer has told them on the albums. They come here wanting something more."

Paisley's show isn't all about video syncs and such, though. As one of the three contemporary country stars who play the majority of their own guitar leads (the others are Keith Urban and Vince Gill), Paisley is eternally fiddling with amp settings and guitar gear. He designs his own amps with equipment maker Dr. Z — the latest is called the Stang Ray — and can talk at length about phase inverters, output transformers and other subjects not normally broached by country artists.

Among the highlights of his tour day is a sound check in which he noodles with equipment and then runs the band through country classics including Merle Haggard's "Sing Me Back Home" and the Ricky Skaggs hit "Highway 40 Blues." And though his concerts follow a set list closely, there is improvisation each night via his guitar work.

Brad Paisley Moves up from Corn Dogs to Catered Meals

"Any given night, I might play great or play bad," he said. "More than likely, there are seven to 10 people out there in the audience who know the difference. But I worry about those seven to 10, and that part helps keep things fresh for me."

After sound check, Paisley worked out with longtime friend and keyboard player Kendal Marcy, who some music fans will recognize as one of the Marcy Brothers. That's the country harmony group that recorded a song called "Don't Break My Heart" in 1991, the same year that the song was re-titled as "Achy Breaky Heart" and recorded by a mullet-wearing Kentuckian named Billy Ray Cyrus. Paisley and Marcy ran for 20 minutes around the center's concourse, then went "off-campus" to a Bally fitness club to lift weights.

He returned in time to prepare for pre-show meet-and-greets, in which he shook hands with fans and local dignitaries. A believer in neatness and hygiene, he washes his hands nearly compulsively, cleans his teeth on the bus with a motorized brush and uses a contraption called "My Little Steamer" to prepare his cowboy hats for the stage.

Early in his career, Paisley's healthy lifestyle and reverence for his country music elders led to the assumption that he was something of a goody two-shoes. To be sure, his tour is free of groupies (he's married to actress Kimberly Williams-Paisley) and his bus contains designer whey and Yoo-hoo chocolate drinks rather than beer, wine or whiskey. But his wit has a decided edge, one that would cause discomfort in someone who was as squeaky clean as Paisley was supposed to be circa 2000.

"Everybody's complicated . . . well, almost everybody," he said. "We all have levels to our personalities, and I have a dark side that's capable of relating to a song like 'Whiskey Lullaby' from heartbreak in the past. I think it took a bunch of songs like that, like 'Celebrity' and some others, to build a persona that was anything like I really am. Nobody likes a practical joke or *South Park* humor more than I do. I hope people realize I'm not a stick-in-the-mud."

After Evans finished her set, Paisley took the stage and delivered a show with plenty of guitar heroics, lots of video, some humor and a set list that includes numerous hit songs. Once he was done, Paisley walked back to the bus with a standing ovation ringing in his ears. He changed clothes, greeted some fans at an after-show function and then met with his band-mates and some crew members for a late night poker session in a backstage room. There were a couple of hours to kill before the buses rolled to Iowa, after all, and the poker table was already set up.

A couple of the poker players swigged beer. Some others sampled late-night liquor.

Paisley shunned the alcohol. He sat there with a big smile on his face, drank a Yoo-hoo and smoked a CAO cigar, smiling like he was winning for sure.

The Godfather of Bluegrass

Even at age 81, banjoist Earl Scruggs is no museum piece

By Jon Weisberger
From *The Nashville Scene*

If the five-string banjo is a cool instrument today – and it undeniably is, with sales of the contraption soaring and its sparkling tones cutting through on a growing number of CDs and concerts by all manner of artists – there is, in the long run, one man to thank. So it's fitting that when the Country Music Hall of Fame and Museum opens the doors to "Banjo Man: The Musical Journey of Earl Scruggs" on March 4, the exhibit will be among the most elaborate the institution has yet devoted to a single artist. And to those who think it celebrates a record of accomplishments that all lie in the distant past, or that belong to one person, the exhibit says, "Think again."

Bluegrass music celebrates its 60th anniversary this year (2005), marking not the date that Bill Monroe put his band together, but the date that Earl Scruggs joined their ranks. As a member of the Blue Grass Boys, Scruggs belonged not only to a group who created a new genre, but to a larger cluster of musicians who were revolutionizing country music in the postwar era. And while Monroe may have the title of "Father of Bluegrass," it was what Scruggs brought to the band that gave the style its most characteristic sound.

Listen to recordings of the Blue Grass Boys' Opry appearances in 1946 and 1947, and it's unmistakable: while audiences were stirred by the group's rapid tempos, high, precise singing and Monroe's stout mandolin playing, it was Earl's banjo solos that drove them into a frenzy. In fact, Scruggs was frequently given co-billing with Monroe by the show's master of ceremonies. "Now here's Bill and Earl, with that fancy banjo," George D. Hay would intone, and the band would be off and running.

That "fancy banjo" had its roots in Cleveland County, N.C., where Scruggs was born in 1924. Though the banjo's role in most rural settings was to provide rhythm for fiddle-led string bands, around Flint Hill there was a small but vital tradition of melody-oriented, three-fingered picking. Raised with his brothers by a mother widowed when he was 4, Earl learned to play on his dad's banjo one of the Hall of Fame exhibit's most significant pieces. By the time he was in his teens, Earl had mastered the local three-fingered tradition and was already moving beyond it, smoothing the uneven style into advanced and rhythmically powerful patterns called "rolls."

"When I came to Nashville, nobody had played the banjo before in that style," Scruggs says. "And I remember, Bill started putting some of the old tunes in the show that really picked good on the banjo. That helped me, to get to play a lot of leading parts. I was getting one or two tunes every Saturday night on the Opry back then. He had 15 minutes by himself, with just one guest, which was Uncle Dave Macon, so he'd get at least four tunes in that 15 minutes, and he'd usually put me on for a tune. So I got a lot of good exposure."

Scruggs and guitarist-lead singer Lester Flatt left Monroe's band at the end of 1947 and, within a matter of weeks, had partnered to form a new band, the Foggy Mountain Boys. Signing with Mercury Records, they recorded 28 sides for the label over the next two years, including what would become one of the most widely recognized tunes in 20th century popular music: "Foggy Mountain Breakdown," Scruggs' tour de force instrumental. Moving to Columbia Records in 1950, they followed a pattern common to many country artists of the period, using a daily radio show to sell songbooks and promote personal appearances within the listening area, then moving to another after "playing out" the territory.

By 1953, they had landed a daily Martha White-sponsored radio show that brought them back to Nashville. By 1955, they were working a weekly, 2,500-mile circuit of TV appearances and concerts that took them from Nashville to Georgia to South Carolina to West Virginia and back again, all the while making increasingly popular records. Thanks to the clout that Martha White's sponsorship gave them, they also were made members of the Grand Ole Opry.

Yet in some ways, the most important thing that happened that year was that Louise Scruggs, Earl's wife of seven years, began to book the band, a job that would grow over the years into the kind of devoted career management that few artists ever have. A Tennessee gal who was working in an accounting firm when she met Scruggs at the Opry, the former Louise Certain had always had an eye for business – indeed, one of the family mementos on display at the Museum is the toy typewriter and desk that she asked for at Christmas one year.

"The rest of the ladies in the neighborhood had little tea parties and bridge games," Louise recalls, "and I wasn't too interested in that. So I was already thinking, 'I think I can do something more. Give me something a little bit more constructive than that.'"

Her opportunity came one day when Scruggs asked her to take care of a booking. "I started out the door one day and gave her a place or two to call," Earl remembers. "Back then, you weren't paid anything to be on radio. You did that to plug your dates and sell songbooks and of course, the Opry didn't pay too much. So concerts were where you made your money.'

"He was trying to book the shows and work, too, so he just didn't have time to do it all," Louise says. "He handed me the name of a person up in Virginia, and he said, 'Here, call this number and see if you can set this concert up with this guy.' So I called him and booked it. Earl got home that night and I said, 'I got you a date booked. Any more names you want me to call?' So he started giving me contacts."

"She liked that," Scruggs says, "and she could get it done much better than me."

Not surprisingly, given the times, she ran into some resistance. "They would always want to talk to Earl, and I'd tell them, 'You're going to have to go through me anyway, so you might as well talk to me now and then we'll get this settled,'" Louise says with a smile. Over the next few years, she took on a bigger role with the group, guiding their career as Flatt & Scruggs and broadening their appeal by reaching out to the emerging folk revival audience.

"I kept up with all the trade paper magazines, and what was going on with the radio stations, and what was getting played," she says. "There wasn't a great difference between what Flatt & Scruggs were already recording and the folk music that was being recorded in that time frame; it just had a different name."

"You'd watch your audience, too," Earl adds. "We got to getting a lot of young people to come when we'd play a park or something, and that would lead you to think that there was another audience out there."

Earl Scruggs: The Godfather of Bluegrass

Louise helped, too, in scoring the group's biggest triumph of the early 1960s, when they recorded the theme song to Hollywood's Beverly Hillbillies television show and then re-recorded it for release as a single. The record shot to No. 1 on the *Billboard* Country chart and reached No. 44 on the Pop chart, though as the Scruggses recall, it nearly didn't happen at all.

"They called and wanted us to do the show, and we turned it down," Earl says with a laugh, "because she couldn't imagine what people in California would make you want to look like as hillbillies. So they sent their music director out here, and they assured us that, yeah, they're going to be real hillbillies, backwoodsmen, but, through common sense, old country common sense, they're going to outsmart the doctors and lawyers. So thats how she put us on the *Beverly Hillbillies*, and that's the way [producer] Paul Henning kept the show; they made everybody look intelligent, at least."

"There are still comments going around, I notice, that that projected a bad image for bluegrass music," Louise notes. "But, my God, it spread it all over the world."

Flatt & Scruggs might have comfortably rode the enduring popularity they'd created for themselves in the early 1960s for the remainder of a long career. For the rest of the decade, they occasionally made it onto the country charts while touring endlessly at home and overseas and making TV appearances, including on their own, long-running syndicated show. Nevertheless, Scruggs was growing restless, spurred by his sons' growing musicianship and his own creativity.

"It started from recording songs," Earl remembers. "Louise had negotiated the new contract with Columbia, and they wanted us to learn some new songs. We had done all that Lester knew how to write, and we just needed some new material — and some of that stuff, Lester's heart just wasn't in it.

"It kind of pulled us apart, I guess. But by that time, [our son] Gary was finishing his four years at Vanderbilt, and Randy had stayed a while at Vanderbilt, but his mind was in music, so I just started up the Revue. Randy and Gary and Steve were one of the biggest influences with me as far as changing and different tunes. They came along with their young ideas; I just went along with the ride, and playing with them was the most enjoyable thing I've ever done. I just went for it, really. I didn't know that it'd do as good as it did."

Though they're amply covered in the "Banjo Man" exhibit, the Revue are not nearly as well remembered as they ought to be these days. Not quite a pioneering country-rock act, they nevertheless served as great popularizers, fusing Earl's banjo licks and, at varying times, the bluegrass-based playing of fiddler Vassar Clements (another former Blue Grass Boy) and Dobro player Josh Graves (a onetime Foggy Mountain Boy) with drums, electric bass, keyboards and electric and acoustic guitars. In the process, they turned signature Scruggs tunes like "Lonesome Reuben" and "Sally Goodin" into extended rave-ups and romped through songs from younger writers like Bob Dylan and Billy Joel.

"That Randy's always been a hot guitar picker," Earl says, "and we put a show together. We'd always open the show with "Nashville Skyline Rag," a tune that Bob Dylan had written, and he'd do the first break with acoustic guitar, and then lay it down and come back with electric guitar on his final break, and he was really cooking when he turned on that electric.

That was kind of the first I'd heard of a real country show that had some rock in it. We weren't shooting for rock 'n' roll at all, but young guys at that time, like Randy and

Gary and Steve, they were fans of it, and they could shove the show right along with that stuff."

While they didn't inspire the same fanaticism that Flatt & Scruggs had engendered among bluegrass fans during their heyday, the Revue were, from a financial point of view, more successful than the Foggy Mountain Boys had ever been. Most notably, they played college campuses and music festivals, where they shared the stage at times with the major rock acts of the day. Still, in the mid-'80s, even as Flatt & Scruggs were inducted into the Country Music Hall of Fame, the Revue disbanded, as Earl began to suffer health problems and Randy pursued a growing career as a session musician and producer. Out of the public eye for the first time in nearly 40 years, by the early '90s Earl Scruggs was beginning to be more of a revered memory than an active participant in the musical scene.

Ironically, it was a health crisis that eventually paved the way for his reemergence. Entering the hospital in 1996 for surgery on a hip replacement he'd had in the 1950s after an auto accident, Scruggs suffered a post-operative heart attack; yet his recovery was such that he wound up feeling better than he had in years. Renewing his interest in picking, he began to take the stage at the Opry again, abetted not only by Randy and Gary, but by a new generation of musicians he'd profoundly influenced, like Vince Gill, Ricky Skaggs and Alison Krauss. He started to make guest appearances on recordings, too, recapping his brilliant guitar picking on "I'm Working on a Road (to Gloryland)" with award-winning bluegrassers IIIrd Tyme Out and contributing to the Grammy-winning "Same Old Train" that closed 1998's star-laden *Tribute to Tradition* compilation.

Freed from the commitment to a full-time band, Scruggs has been giving free reign to his interests, including finding young musicians with whom to play, both onstage with his Family and Friends outfit and at "pickin's" held at the Scruggs home. "He likes to pick with young people," Louise says. "They're always coming up with some innovative idea or lick. It turns him on, too, so he'll go and play something crazy that they haven't heard, and they'll come offstage saying, 'Did you hear what Earl played? I never heard him do that before!'"

At the same time, he's been collaborating with a variety of heavyweights from other genres, as he did on *2001's Earl Scruggs and Friends*, which features guest turns by country stars like Gill, Johnny Cash and Marty Stuart, as well as from pop and rock figures like Sting and Melissa Etheridge.

Though the album's star-studded remake of "Foggy Mountain Breakdown" earned Scruggs a Grammy the following year, the disc itself got a mixed reaction. For those prizing rootsiness as a musical ideology, the presence of pop stars like Elton John and Don Henley was, it seems, hard to swallow. For Earl, though — presumably inured to such criticism since his break with Flatt in 1969 — making the album was a thoroughly satisfying experience. His enthusiasm, the ultimate key to his stature, is evident throughout the album, suggesting that his journey isn't yet over.

"Boy, that was a joyful thing to do," he says. "I guess the first one we did was with Elton, at a studio down there in north Georgia. When he came in and hit that piano, golly, it was just like the whole room was full of piano.

"What little jump in show business I've done is because of getting to play with different people like that. I just always felt that if I didn't play something besides the eight or 10 bluegrass tunes that we'd been doing —if I didn't play something else, I was just depriving myself of enjoyment in life. And I just knew that my style of playing the banjo could fit in with what other people were doing. So I just went for it. I just felt like I owed it to myself to do something with those guys."

Why George Is Still On Top

Twenty-five years into his amazing career, George Strait is still setting the standard for straight-ahead country—and is still revered as the "King"

By David Scarlett
From *Country Weekly*

In 1981, George Strait released his first single, "Unwound," and watched it climb to the Top 10 on the Country charts. Now, a quarter century later, George has scored more than 50 No. 1 hits (all charts combined)—from "Fool Hearted Memory" and "The Chair" to "You Look So Good in Love" and "Write This Down"—and he's *still* performing sold-out shows at large venues all over the country.

George won yet another CMA award—his 13th—in November for his "Good News, Bad News" duet with Lee Ann Womack. And the superstar has been nominated nearly 70 times!

Each of his more than 30 albums has gone at least gold, and many have achieved multiplatinum status. "You'll Be There," from his current *Somewhere Down in Texas* CD, had the highest charting debut week of his career at No. 30.

And the CD entered the Billboard 200 pop charts at No. 1. Now the album's second single, "She Let Herself Go," is nearing the top of the charts.

Younger country artists, almost without exception, cite George as a major influence on their music. And not just *any* younger artists—everyone from Garth Brooks and Tim McGraw to Dierks Bentley, Joe Nichols and Miranda Lambert has given George his due as someone they admire—as much for the quiet, confident way he carries himself as for the way he sings.

When Miranda learned she'd been invited to open for George on his 2006 tour, she was beyond excited. "I'm so honored that George would take a chance on a new artist like me," she grins. "I feel kind of like the little girl whose daddy just said 'I'm proud of you, you're gonna make it, kid!' I've admired him my whole life and, as a singer/songwriter from Texas, it's like winning the lottery."

But *why*?

What is it about this 53-year-old Poteet, Texas, native that makes him so beloved by fans and fellow musicians alike that he has been dubbed "King George"? It's certainly not his onstage fireworks or the scantily-clad women in his videos—he has none of those. It's also not his endless publicity seeking—George keeps a notoriously low profile, rarely granting interviews and only occasionally posing for photos to promote his own records and tours.

What about trend-setting fashion choices? Nope—he's worn starched Wrangler jeans and shirts, boots and cowboy hat his entire career. Nothing flashy there.

And scandal? Never the slightest hint. He's the quintessential good guy who treats everyone with respect, and he's just as in love with wife Norma today as when they eloped as high school sweethearts more than 35 years ago.

George records an album every year and does about 25

Why George Is Still On Top

tour dates annually—that's it. The rest of the time he spends living his non-show biz life with Norma on his ranch near San Antonio, Texas, and enjoying his passion for riding and team calf roping. But having a 25-date tour schedule isn't as easy to do as it might sound. There's a lot of pressure for hit artists to travel throughout the year, doing at least 100 shows. But one of the luxuries of being George Strait is having the clout to dictate your own schedule.

Dierks, who's opened for George on each of his past two tours, does more than 200 dates a year, so he has a great appreciation for George's decision to scale back his time on the road. "He's been doing this since, I think, the mid-'80s," declares Dierks. "He just said, 'You know what? Six months out of the year I want to be out there makin' music and makin' records. The other six months, I'm not gonna see my guitar. I'm gonna put it in the closet and just stay on the ranch.'

"He kind of just drew the line and kept his life—which is really admirable."

And that may be at least part of George's appeal. He comes across in his music as what he is in real life—a genuine Texas cowboy who sings about what he knows, without airs and without compromising who he is. His "take me as I am" musical philosophy led him to keep his cowboy hat when Nashville music executives told him early in his career he'd be better off without it. He's still got *his* hat—and some of those execs have been handed theirs.

George steadfastly refuses to record music that's not right for him, even if it might broaden his appeal to crossover pop audiences. But what's "right" for him sometimes isn't easy for others to predict.

George has a great ear for what'll work, and he leans strongly toward traditional country. But every now and then he'll do a song that pushes the boundaries a little . . .

songs like "Run," the Top 5 hit from his 2001 *The Road Less Traveled* CD. Musically, the tune sounds decidedly more pop than a lot of George's other hits, but that Strait voice and strong lyric make it work for him.

It's that willingness to stretch the parameters without betraying who he is that keeps George relevant for newer, younger audiences. And, because they like his *new* stuff, they'll go see him and be exposed to some of the older songs that may have inspired George—maybe a Bob Wills tune or a Lefty Frizzell song. As Dierks once said, George is a very important "bridge" from contemporary country music to the music of some of country's founding fathers.

Teenagers stand and yell for him while their parents and grandparents smile and tap their feet approvingly. George doesn't dance around the stage. He and his incredible Ace in the Hole band just stand and deliver—one excellent performance after another. Show after show, year after year.

And, perhaps, when you get right down to it, that's at the core of George's success as much as anything. He is one gifted singer who surrounds himself with great people, treats them well and absolutely loves what he does. His fans and fellow artists know he's the "real deal" and they appreciate the integrity he brings to everything he does—onstage and off.

And, although he's given no hint that he's ready to hang up the guitar for good, if and when he does . . . his fans will know where to find him. A few lines of the title tune from his *Somewhere* CD sum it up pretty nicely:

I'll be somewhere down in Texas if you're lookin' for me
Drinkin' in that great wide-open, soakin' up the summer breeze
Kickin' back an' settled in with my family
I'll be somewhere down in Texas if you're lookin' for me

Sounds good to us, George. Just don't make it any time soon.

Just What the Hell Is Country Music, Anyway?

By Chet Flippo
From "Nashville Skyline" column
CMT.com

Right. Just what the hell is country music these days, anyhow? I'm getting asked that a lot these days, and so are some of my friends who are in the habit of commenting publicly on music. Over-exposed actresses decide they need to display their country roots on record, aging rockers come to Nashville for a country blood transfusion and fading actors suddenly decide they've "always been country."

I can tell you that, like the classic definition of pornography, I know what country is when I hear it. Like hearing young newcomer Ray Scott's authoritative vocal delivery on a gritty new song like the title cut from his upcoming CD, *My Kind of Music*. And you know what is not country when you hear it. Like Jessica Simpson singing "These Boots Are Made for Walkin'."

Let me give you a little musical vignette. CDs by Neil Young, Lori McKenna, Wayne Scott (no relation to Ray Scott) and a new tribute to the Bailes Brothers are the most played CDs in my office and car players right now. These works are very different yet very much alike in many ways.

Are they country? Yes. Well, who says so? Who certifies what is country and what is not? And, in fact, these days what exactly is country music? Just who is a country artist? Good questions. Easy to ask. Harder to answer.

Country attitudes and point of view define the musical point of view, along with a certain compassion and sincerity and conviction. The music, after all, came out of folk music and blues and gospel, all of which are peer group musical forms. Music that's created for one's neighbors and friends, not for a giant corporation. Ideally, it is music of the people for the people. It is also a music genre that still honors its founders and pioneers and its historical legacy.

But, musical artists need to make a living. So there is commercial country, referred to these days as mainstream or even radio country or Big Box country, after the huge discount stores where most of the CDs are sold. There's no reason to assume commercial country cannot be great country music, and it sometimes is.

Traditionally country has been rural based and continues to be so in outlook. The music's moral foundations remain in the country, even as its musical forms and lyrics migrate toward city rhythms and themes. But the overriding themes continue to be family, friends, fellow man, faith and patriotism. And, of course, good times. Texas singer-songwriter Jack Ingram has a good definition of what country music knows about good times. The music tells you you're having a good time, he says. And the lyrics tell you *why* we need to have a good time.

Neil Young has long embraced the country tradition and made overtly country albums such as *Harvest and Harvest Moon*. He returned to Nashville to cut the gorgeous, understated, very country CD *Prairie Wind* that pays tribute to his Canadian rural heritage and to his late father. He also filmed a DVD of the work at Nashville's Ryman Auditorium, a concert that remains one of the finest I have ever seen and heard.

So, is Neil Young country? Hell yes, he is, when he's writing and singing superb songs from his heart such as these.

Wayne Scott has just released his first album—at age 71. And it's a pretty damned good chronicle of a way of life that's passing from the American scene. The life of the raw-boned, strong, blue-collar laborer who raises a family to aspire to a better life than he has known and does the best he can. I'll let his son, the great singer-songwriter Darrell Scott, describe this man and this album: *"This Weary Way* has been a long time coming—an album of original songs by my dad—Wayne Scott. Growing up on a tobacco farm in Crane's Nest, Ky., in the '30s and '40s, the 11th of 13 children, four themes fill his stories—work, family, church and music, in that order. This recording may be a proud and thankful son helping to document his father's lifework. It is both the least and most that I could do." It is not a pretty album, but that's not what country music should always be. It's real, and is what it is.

I've already written in this space about singer-songwriter Lori McKenna and her superb work, *Bittertown*. I'm beginning to think it's the single best CD I've heard this year from any genre of music, let alone country. And it's all about real life and emotions and human drama; all things that the best country songs have always embraced. McKenna's writing and singing are country music emotion laid on the line for all to see and hear and feel.

Bill Malone is the pre-eminent historian of country music. His pioneering book, *Country Music U.S.A.*, is the main reason country music began to be taken seriously as an art form.

Now he and his fellow retired folklorist and historian Rod Moag are doing what they can to preserve and advance the musical legacy of the sadly neglected Bailes Brothers with their CD *Remember Me: Bill Malone & Rod Moag Play the Music of the Bailes Brothers*. They have sung duets of 19 of the Bailes' most memorable songs, and they were aided by the likes of steel guitar players Lloyd Maines and Cindy Cashdollar recreating the classic sound of Shot Jackson, the classic steel player who was an integral part of the Bailes' sound. They also got vocal help from the only surviving Bailes Brother, the elderly Homer Bailes.

The Bailes epitomized the music of post-World War II America, when the rural way of life underwent a major upheaval with a massive shift of workers moving from the farm to factory and other industrial jobs in the cities. The Bailes' music, as Malone points out in his liner notes, helped "remind us of where we came from, [and] they also conveyed the strength of our common culture and helped us to survive in a new and unfamiliar world." Perhaps the Bailes' best-known song, especially as popularized by Willie Nelson with his version on his *Red Headed Stranger* album is the song "Remember Me," with its well-known refrain:

"Remember me when the candle lights are gleaming/Remember me at the close of a long, long day / And it would be so sweet when all alone, I'm dreaming / Just to know you still remember me."

Malone and Moag are not overly pretty or slick slingers, but it sounds beautiful, as only true music, sung with conviction, can sound.

ALECIA NUGENT

By Geoffrey Himes
From *Bluegrass Unlimited*

In 1992, Alecia Nugent was not a budding bluegrass star, with her second Rounder album coming out, as she is today. Back then she was just a skinny, 20-year-old beauty, a single mother with a daughter and a special soprano that few outside of Louisiana had ever heard.

One of those few was Bertie Sullivan, the Mississippi bluegrass promoter who thought Nugent was so good that she needed to meet some real music pros up close and personal. So Sullivan invited her young friend to a concert at the Hattiesburg Elks Lodge, where Carl Jackson, Larry Cordle, Jerry Salley and Jim Rushing were playing their songs in an old-fashioned guitar pull.

Nugent found a babysitter, drove over to Mississippi and found the four men sitting in chairs in a semi-circle, an acoustic guitar on each right thigh, taking turns to sing their songs. When Jackson sang "My Girl Friday," the story of a divorced father who can only see his daughter on Fridays, Nugent was reduced to tears.

"I had just gone through a divorce," she remembers, "so I knew what that song was all about. Even though I had custody of my daughter, I knew what it was like to wait for that certain day to be with her. I knew the pain of being separated from your spouse and child.

"It wasn't till that night that I understood the impact that a bluegrass or country song can have on a person.

When you hear someone put your own experiences into a song, you're able to put all the mistakes you've made into perspective. It's like you've relived it. A song can be like therapy, because hearing it can make you face reality in that moment. It was such a powerful feeling that I knew that that's what I wanted to do with my life."

That epiphany opened up the pipeline between Nugent's emotional life and her music and led to one of the most promising careers in bluegrass today. For her, bluegrass is not about remembering a simpler time or paying tribute to a previous generation; it's about facing the reality of the here and now. It's not about hot solos; it's about helping all those small-town, working-class Southerners born since 1970 make sense of their lives.

It's about reflecting back the lives of all those young women who work in front of computers all day, pick up their kids at day care and go home to think up new ways to use hamburger helper. It's about bringing all their buried frustrations and longings to the surface. Nugent can connect with that audience, because she is that audience.

Later that evening in Hattiesburg, her eyes now dry, Nugent ascended the stage and sang "Amazing Grace" with Jackson and Cordle. She returned with the performers to Sullivan's house and they stayed up all night, picking and singing. Jackson and his pals complimented and encouraged her, and she thought, hey, maybe someone outside Louisiana might be interested in my singing. They told her to stay in touch and she did.

"I had never heard of Alecia," Jackson admits, "but Bertie said, 'I want you to hear this girl sing.' So we brought Alecia up and when she sang 'Amazing Grace,' she absolutely blew me away. She had this thing about her voice that's so heartrending and so lonesome. She knew when to sing soft, when to sing hard and when to put that quiver in her voice. So many people sing for you and you say they sound like this singer or that singer. But Alecia sounded like herself, right from the first time I heard her."

Jackson wound up producing both of Nugent's solo albums, and the second one, *A Little Girl ... A Big Four-Lane*, has just been released. He plays the Scruggs-like banjo and sings the harmony on the album's lead-off track, "Too Good To Be True," written by Larry Cordle and Leslie Satcher.

"In a '68 Camaro, a little girl, a big four-lane," Nugent sings, her soprano skipping like a stone, "oh, she's flying like an arrow, out across the Pontchartrain." The character in the song is a 21-year-old small town girl running off to meet an older man in New Orleans who has promised a life of mansions and parties down on St. Charles Avenue.

But by the end of the song, the young protagonist is singing, "If it sounds too good to be true, it probably is." If Nugent seems to be singing from deep inside the song, it's because the song's character is more than a little like Nugent herself, who grew up in Hickory Grove, Louisiana, and wound up a wife and a mother right after high school.

"Being a small-town Louisiana girl, that song struck home," she admits. "In both of my marriages, promises were made that were too good to be true. I know how it is to be an only daughter and have your dad tell you to be careful as a young woman. I know how it is to fall for promises anyway and have those promises broken. I know how it is to be out on my own as a result."

Two more songs on the new album capture the tug-of-war between small-town roots and big-city ambitions. On "God Knows What," Nugent sings of driving away from Hickory Grove and heading for Nashville, searching for "God knows what." If Adam Steffey's mandolin chop represents the urge for going, Jim Van Cleve's melancholy fiddle lines signify the second thoughts.

On "Letter from Home," she sings of how a hand-written letter from her parents can spark both a smile of memory and an ache of homesickness. If the smile is echoed in Steve Sutton's banjo, the ache is reflected in Rob Ickes' Dobro.

"It helps to sing songs like 'God Knows What' and 'Letter from Home,'" Nugent confesses. "They give you words for what you want to express. I'm a very reserved person; I don't talk about my feelings very much, so if I can sing it in a song, that's my way of expressing it. In a conversation, when it's one-on-one, I might have trouble getting the words out. But when I'm standing there singing a song, I'm singing it to myself; I'm not actually telling it to somebody else.

"A song means more if I've experienced it. There's a line in 'Letter from Home' about her dad pulling off on the side on the radio to hear her on the radio, and that actually happened one time when I appeared on the Grand Ole Opry. My dad couldn't go, so he was driving along the road trying to pick up the signal 'till he got to the top of the hill and pulled over."

"The first number-one song I ever had was 'Letter to Home,' which Glen Campbell recorded," Jackson points out. "I thought it would be fun to turn it around and write a song called 'Letter from Home.' I wrote it with Jennifer McCarter 14 years ago and the McCarters recorded it. The line that was "a picture of life in Mississippi" when I sang it became "a picture of life in the mountains" when Jennifer sang it and became "a picture of life in Louisiana" when Alecia sang it. That's just one example of how we altered some lyrics to make the songs more personal for Alecia so she could get deeper inside them."

In 1972, the year Nugent was born, her father Jimmy

Nugent, a machinist, formed the Southland Bluegrass Band in Hickory Grove, a tiny town 20 miles northeast of Alexandria, Louisiana. Ray Nugent, Jimmy's second cousin, played mandolin, and Ray's son Dickie played bass (and now does the same for Larry Stephenson; Dickie's son Tres now plays bass for Special Consensus). Alecia's mother Carolyn, a secretary, played piano at the Holloway Baptist Church.

"All I knew growing up was bluegrass festivals, pickings at our house and Ray's house and Fifth Sunday singings where we'd sing hymns all day," she recalls. "My mom's dad was music director at his church, and my dad's dad was music director at his church. I think it made a big difference growing up that way. Listening to all that old music gave me the sound I have today. If I'd just started listening to bluegrass in college, I don't think it would have been the same.

"I became the lead singer for my dad's band when I was 15," she adds. "He was a big advocate of singing with the power coming from the diaphragm, not the throat, just like his heroes Carter Stanley and Larry Sparks. He'd have us go into the bathroom to practice our harmonies so they sounded right. To sound right they had to sound like a car horn—big, full and powerful. My dad wouldn't have it any other way."

During her junior high, Alecia inevitably discovered pop music and became a fan of Madonna, Michael Jackson and Deborah Allen. In high school she turned to hard-rock bands such as AC/DC, Bon Jovi and Def Leppard. Her father would let her listen to whatever she wanted as long as he wasn't in the room.

But even when she got married and pregnant right after high school, even when she got divorced in 1991, remarried in 1994 and divorced again in 2001, she kept singing with the Southland Bluegrass Band. She helped them record the album *Big House on the Corner* in 1990 and Southland's *Amazing Grace* in 1994.

"My biggest musical influence is my dad," she claims, "and his influences are Flatt & Scruggs, Larry Sparks and Bill Monroe, so that rubbed off on me. The engineer on my first album said, 'Are you sure you're from Louisiana and not from Virginia?' I said, 'Yes, I'm sure.' So he called me a swampbilly.

"Reba McEntire and Patty Loveless were my biggest female influences, them and Rhonda Vincent. I met Rhonda when she was playing with the Sally Mountain Band. Her family played my grandfather's festival, which was right in my backyard, the Hickory Grove Music Festival at the Hickory Grove Music Park."

"Rhonda and Alecia were both able to develop more quickly because they were in family bands," Jackson argues. "Just getting out there every weekend taught them more than they ever could have gotten from school or lessons.

"I know, because my dad and my two uncles had a band, the Country Partners, that I joined when I first started playing banjo at eight or nine, way before I went with Jim & Jesse. Sometimes you wonder if you hadn't been born into the right family and if you hadn't gotten that extra push what might have happened. Alecia's dad was like my dad; bluegrass is number one for both of them. They want nothing more than to see you sitting around practicing bluegrass."

Through all the ups and downs of her personal life, Nugent kept singing bluegrass and stayed in touch with Jackson. Her family's band rarely left Louisiana and never farther than Mississippi or Arkansas, so few bluegrass fans got a chance to hear her. But one of those who did, Mississippi promoter Johnny Stringer, was so impressed that he offered to finance her debut solo album.

With that money in hand, she finally got to make the phone call she'd so often dreamed of. She called up Jackson and asked if he'd produce her first album. He quickly agreed and got to work looking for songs.

"I knew we wanted to do some standards," he remembers, "because it's a good way to introduce a new act. You want to prove that they can not only handle the new stuff but can also handle the old stuff and know their place in the tradition. The Stanley Brothers' 'Think of What You Done' hadn't been done by a girl, so that gave it a new twist.

"There were a couple of things she wanted to do, and Stringer really wanted her to do Tex Ritter's 'Jealous Heart,' which was fine because I loved the song. Then we started looking through my catalogue, Larry's catalogue and Jerry's catalogue to find the right songs for her."

The album was released in 2001 as *For Love's Sake* by Alecia McRight, her married name at the time. Featuring an all-star band that included Jackson, fiddler Aubrey Haynie, mandolinist Ronnie McCoury, dobroist Randy Kohrs and bassist Ben Isaacs, with harmony vocals by Jackson, Rhonda Vincent, Larry Cordle, Sonya Isaacs and Jimmy Nugent, the disc attracted more attention than the usual self-released debut. Nugent soon found herself playing outside her accustomed Louisiana-Mississippi-Arkansas circuit.

As she did, however, she encountered more than a little skepticism. Some bluegrass audiences, it seemed, were unwilling to accept a lead singer who didn't play an instrument—especially a woman with a model's good looks. Nugent had the chiseled cheekbones, the dark, shoulder-length red hair and the long, slender frame that made people wonder if they were responding to the audio or the visual.

"I know for a fact that some people have judged me on

the basis of my looks before getting to know me," Nugent laments. "I've had people tell me that when they first saw the cover of my CD, they said, 'Oh just another pretty face; they're trying to sell her looks because she can't sing that well.' But when they listened, they were surprised. They say, 'I can't believe that big voice comes out of such a little person.'

"It still bothers me when I hear people say, 'Why don't you play an instrument on stage?'" Nugent adds. "I feel my voice is my instrument. I never had the ambition to learn another instrument, so I've always concentrated on my vocal abilities. My dad used to tell me that a band is only as good as its weakest link. If I can't play as well as my band, why should I stand up there as the weakest link?"

"It's still unusual to have a bluegrass singer who doesn't play an instrument," Jackson says, "but she carries her weight so well as a vocalist that it doesn't matter. It doesn't bother me, but I know it bothers some people. But once you hear her sing, I think that goes out the window."

Amid the skeptics, there were some true believers, and one of them was Ken Irwin, co-owner of Rounder Records. He signed Nugent to his label and re-released her debut album with a new title, *Alecia Nugent*, in 2004. Moreover, he put two of the album's tracks on Rounder compilations (*O Sister 2: A Women's Bluegrass Collection* and *White Dove: The Bluegrass Gospel Collection*) and placed Nugent's new recording of "Beautiful Star of Bethlehem" on "O Christmas Tree: A Bluegrass Collection for the Holidays."

But things didn't get any easier for Nugent. Her second divorce led to a messy custody battle. At first she tried to move to Nashville in 2002 with her three daughters (Meagan, who's now 14; Santanna, who's now 10; and Breanna, who's now 9). But when a Louisiana judge nixed that plan, she moved back to Hickory Ridge in 2003 and has bounced back and forth between the two towns ever since. Like many women of her generation, she finds herself torn between her kids and her career, loving both too much to sacrifice either.

"Home is important to me," she insists. "Louisiana is where my family is. I've had a lot of heartache and pain there, but being able to move on has made me a better person. I can look back and appreciate the experiences I had there. I've actually left home twice to come to Nashville and try to do music."

All that personal drama lends an emotional charge to everything Nugent sings on the new album, especially the songs about troubled relationships. On "When It Comes Down to Us," a woman resolves to keep trying to make a relationship work despite all the failures in the past. On "Muddy River," a woman realizes she has to let the past go like debris washed away in a flood if she's to move forward with her life.

On "It Won't Be Me," a woman tells a departing man to not even think about coming back. On "Breaking New Ground," a woman tells her ex-lover that she's starting over with someone new. And on "You've Still Got It," a woman desperately tries to break things off with a lover but finds she can't resist his lingering charms.

"I've been through those relationships," Nugent says of the last song, "where you know the best thing is to not be together, but you can't let go of those feelings because that person still holds a special place in your heart. Everybody's been through something like that. I liked the lyrics, but mostly I liked the melody and the chord progressions, which are very interesting, very different. I've always loved that kind of stuff, but I've never sung it, and I wanted to give it a shot."

"'You've Still Got It' is a little different direction for

Alecia," Jackson suggests, "because she's not singing in the power mode. It's not what you'd call a typical Alecia song, because she sings so softly. But Alecia is more versatile than people think. We brought in Alison Krauss to sing on this track, and Alecia held her own."

Other guest singers on the album include Doyle Lawson, Cia Cherryholmes and Rebecca Lynn Howard. But the one full-fledged duet finds Nugent singing the honky-tonk confession, "When It Comes Down to Us," with Bradley Walker. Walker, who is working with Jackson on his solo debut album for Rounder Records, boasts the kind of authoritative baritone that makes you forget about his wheelchair and unusual back story.

"Bradley and I have been good friends ever since we met at the 2001 IBMA and had the chance to sing together," Nugent explains. "We've stayed in touch on almost a daily basis, and he's become one of my favorite singing partners. I love the deepness of his voice; it reminds me of Keith Whitley and George Jones, the ability to go down as deep as he can go and still sing with feeling. Certain moves he makes when he's singing give me chill bumps."

At last October's IBMA, Nugent previewed the songs from her second album. Backed by her road band (mandolinist Darren Nicholson, banjoist Steve Sutton, bassist Jennifer Strickland and guitarist Andy Falco) she ripped through "Too Good To Be True" with a confidence only hinted at on her first album. Wearing big silver hoop earrings and a shimmery brown blouse, she milked the slower songs "God Knows What" and "Letter From Home" for every drop of drama.

"The prettier the melody, the easier the song is for me to sing," she notes. "Maybe that's why I'm such a ballad lover. A strong melody allows you to be soft at times and to be powerful at other times. I especially like melodies that show the mood changing during the same song.

"Some may say those melodies are too country or too pop, but if we want to keep bluegrass alive, we have to keep the younger generation interested. I record the kind of music that feels like me, the kind I think people in my generation will be able to relate to. I can't play a hot solo, so I have to have a good story and a pretty melody that I can sing."

Women Make Inroads into Realm of Record Production

Veteran artists step up from calling their own shots to steering creative process for others

By Peter Cooper
From *The Tennessean*

Lari White just produced a Toby Keith album called *White Trash With Money*. It sold more than 400,000 copies in less than a month and is expected to spawn several country radio hits.

And that shouldn't be all that surprising a deal. Keith is, after all, among country's biggest stars. He had the most-played country radio song of the 1990s with "Should've Been a Cowboy," he's been a well-known commercial commodity in the new century and he's well known for his ability to win fans with attitude-laden, "love-me-or-loathe-me" recordings.

But the whole thing is surprising, not so much because of Keith's popularity and longevity, and not solely because this is Keith's first release on his own record label. The whole thing is most surprising because of the gender of the producer. Women, it seems, don't normally produce hit albums for male country artists.

In fact, until this new Toby Keith song-set, a woman has never produced a hit album for a contemporary country superstar male artist. The person who oversees the recording process, determines which musicians will play, guides the superstar country artist through the sessions and in the end reaps a chunk of the sales proceeds has never, until White, been a woman.

A position that requires no brute strength and is most capably handled by people with good interpersonal skills, advanced listening abilities and broad musical knowledge, "producer" would not seem to be a job that would be the near sole domain of men.

"It's odd that it's odd for a woman to do this, isn't it?" White mused. "In all kinds of professions, though, women are still playing catch-up, and it's probably going to take many more years."

The Jackie Robinson of Music City female producers is Gail Davies, who kicked down Music Row doors in 1979 by producing her own *The Game* album, which was released in 1980. Before that, Davies fought battle after battle in trying to assert herself in the studio with male producers and musicians.

"I met with unbelievable opposition," she said. "They treated me like (expletive). Men have changed tremendously in country music in the last 30 years, and even then there were some men who were very supportive of what I was trying to do. But it's like (California session bass player) Leland Sklar said once, 'When Gail Davies came to Nashville, women were still barefoot, pregnant and in the vocal booth.'"

Not that country is much less inclusive than pop, rock

or R&B, though the sheer volume of output in those genres has helped at least some women wind up with production credit.

In the 1980s and 1990s, several Nashville women followed Davies' cue. Wendy Waldman produced music for New Grass Revival, Suzy Bogguss and others, Pam Tillis produced her own work, and the Nashville duo of Mary Ann Kennedy and Pam Rose produced their records for Sting's Pangaea Records.

With the exception of Waldman, though, women who produced almost always did so only for their own albums. Davies' 1990s efforts as country's first female staff producer (meaning she worked for the label to produce other artists) at Jimmy Bowen's Liberty label were more frustrating than fruitful. She claims she was squashed by Bowen, who she said assigned her to record demos for newbie acts in an effort to "see whether they were ready to make albums."

"So many aspects of this business are just seen as male," said Martina McBride, who produced her most recent album, *Timeless*. "I don't know why that is. I just feel like it's automatically thought of as a male position. I think even when women do produce their own albums, some people think, 'Yeah right, she just put her name on it and there was a man there who did all the work.'"

White, Davies, Rose, hit songwriter/would-be producer Victoria Shaw and much-celebrated producer Buddy Cannon (he's the chief on Kenny Chesney's multi-million-selling albums) cited numerous factors that have hindered the number of women in the position.

Lack of female role models, the still-short history of women producers in Nashville and the glaring lack of any female record label heads in town are three points that were brought up repeatedly in conversation. Label leaders are often quite active as producers on their labels and for artists on other labels. Paul Worley, Tony Brown, Luke Lewis and James Stroud are among Music Row kingpins who guide companies and who produce artists, and these men have no female corporate peers in Nashville. So those slots are filled, and other producers aren't likely to freely cede ground.

"I remember when I was wanting to break into production: It's such a protected job," Cannon said. "Other producers don't want to let anybody new in, not just women. They're afraid for their job security."

Rose, who owns her own recording studio and who has written hit songs for McBride, Restless Heart and others, is hoping White's work with Keith will contribute to a change in the atmosphere.

"Toby is a secure artist and a secure man, obviously, and he's in a position to say creatively, 'This is who I think I'll make the best music with.' Every one of the guys who is a top producer had to be given a chance at some point. Maybe it's time now that some of the people given that first chance are women, if they're talented enough and capable enough."

Another hit songwriter, Victoria Shaw, is also seeking an opportunity to produce a major artist. "I don't waste my time moaning about how it's so much harder for a woman, but it is a fact that when you look at the country charts, until this Toby album, you don't often see women producers listed there. Now that Lari has made history, it's going to open doors for everybody. It took a brave man, and Toby is a brave chance-taker. I think he'll go down in history as someone who really changed things."

Another country superstar will soon join what is now Keith's one-member club: Alan Jackson has lately been in the studio working on sessions produced by acoustic music luminary Alison Krauss.

"Things are better now," said Davies, who in 2002 produced each of the 21 tracks on *Caught in the Webb*, a tribute to Webb Pierce that featured Emmylou Harris, George Jones, Willie Nelson and Dwight Yoakam among many others. "And I think there'll be girls coming up who are going to want to do this. I lectured at a couple of colleges and talked to roomfuls of kids about production. I told the girls, 'If you want to produce, you don't have to learn how to do everything. You have to learn how to know who works together well and how to put things together.'"

For her part, White has been answering questions from journalists, friends and others about her groundbreaking role in Keith's album. She has yet to tire of the queries.

"I'm happy to talk about it to help continue the motion of women in this world," she said. "The more we can get it out there and open people's minds to it, the more natural it will become."

Peter Cooper

CONTRIBUTORS

Peter Cooper covers music for the *Tennessean* newspaper in Nashville.

Peter Cronin is the editor of *CMA Close Up* magazine. He has also worked as the media director and editor of the SESAC magazine, *Focus*, and has been the creative director at Bug Music in Nashville.

Bill DeMain is a contributing writer for several music publications and the author of *In Their Own Words: Songwriters Talk About the Creative Process*. He lives in Nashville.

Bob Doerschuk is an accomplished jazz pianist and a co-author of *88: The Giants of Jazz Piano*.

Chet Flippo is the author of *It's only Rock and Roll: My On-the-Road Adventures with the Rolling Stones, Your Cheatin' Heart (A Biography of Hank Williams)* and other books on music. He also writes the "Nashville Skyline" column for the CMT.com website.

Thomas Goldsmith is features editor for the *News and Observer* in Raleigh, North Carolina, and the editor of *The Bluegrass Reader*. Previously, he was assistant managing editor for the *Tennessean* in Nashville.

Geoffrey Himes lives in Baltimore and is the author of

Contributors

Born in the U.S.A. (biography of Bruce Springsteen). He is a past winner of the Deems-Taylor award for music feature writing, and also composed the musical, *A Baltimore Christmas Carol.*

John Hood is a contributing writer for numerous websites and publications, including *Music City News, CMA Close-Up,* and *Cybergrass Bluegrass Music News.*

Rick Kelly is a native Nashvillian who has spent his career working in the country music industry. His primary areas of interest as a writer are classic artists from the 1960'-1970's, and the songwriters and instrumentalists who fuel the Nashville music industry.

Michael McCall is an editor for the *Journal of Country Music* and has written for *The Nashville Scene, Country Music,* and many other music publications.

Alanna Nash is an award-winning music journalist and the author of *The Colonel: The Extraordinary Story of Colonel Tom Parker and Elvis Presley, Dolly* (a biography of Dolly Parton), *Elvis and the Memphis Mafia,* and *Golden Girl: The Story of Jessica Savitch.*

Danny Proctor has been an art director for *Advantage, Tennessee Business, Christian Woman, Music City News* and a freelance journalist for such publications as *Country Weekly, Music City News, Tune-In,* and the website BMI.com.

Chris Stuart is a writer and songwriter based in San Diego and founder of the bluegrass band Chris Stuart & Backcountry.

Contributors

Josh Tyrangiel is a music critic for *Time* magazine and has written feature stories on rock legends Bruce Springsteen, Bono, and others.

Tom Roland is a veteran music writer and author of *The Billboard Book Of #1 Country Hits*. A former critic for *The Tennessean*, his work has also appeared in *The Hollywood Reporter, The Orange County Register* and *USA Weekend*, and he's written numerous national radio programs for Westwood One and the United Stations Radio Networks.

David Scarlett has spent more than 20 years as a performer/songwriter, public relations executive and writer. He is now a now senior editor for *Country Weekly* magazine.

Bill Friskics-Warren is a veteran music journalist and has written for *The Nashville Scene, USA Today, The Washington Post*, and many other publications. He is the author of *I'll Take You There: Pop Music and the Urge for Transcendence* and a co-author of *Heartaches by the Number: Country Music's 500 Greatest Singles*.

Jon Weisberger has earned two IBMA awards ("Print Media Person of the Year in 2000" and "Best Liner Notes" for John Duffey's *Always In Style*), and is an accomplished bluegrass musician as well.

PERMISSIONS

"Rosanne Cash Shares Her Pain," written by Peter Cooper, originally appeared in the Nashville *Tennessean* on April 16, 2006. Reprinted by permission of the *Tennessean*.

"Emmylou Harris & Mark Knopfler: The Road Runs from Nashville to Notting Hill" by Bill DeMain, originally appeared in *Performing Songwriter* in the May, 2006 issue. Reprinted by permission of the author and *Performing Songwriter*

"The Dixie Chicks: In the Line of Fire" by Josh Tyrangiel, originally appeared as the cover story in *Time* on May 29, 2006. Reprinted by permission from *Time*.

"It Was the Singing: A Conversation with Mac Wiseman," by Thomas Goldsmith, originally appeared in B*luegrass Unlimited* in the February, 2006 issue. Reprinted by permission of the publication and author.

"Carrie Underwood's Wild Ride" by Peter Cronin, was originally published in the June/July 2006 issue of *CMA Close Up*. Reprinted by permission of the publication and the author.

"Matraca Berg: Pensive Behind the Pen" by Robert L. Doerschuk, originally appeared in *American Songwriter* in the June 2006 issue. Reprinted by permission of the author.

"George Jones" by Danny Proctor, originally appeared in *Music City News* in the September 2005 issue. Reprinted by permission of Music City News.

"To Beat the Devil: Intimations of Immortality" (Kris Kristoferson) by Bill Friskics-Warren, originally appeared in *No Depression* in the March/April 2006 issue. Reprinted by permission of the author.

"Buck Owens: 1929-2006" by Tom Roland, originally appeared in *Country Weekly* on April 24, 2006. Reprinted by permission of the author.

"Climbing to the Top of the Duo Heap: An Interview With Troy Gentry," by John Hood, originally appeared in *Music City News* in the February 2006 issue. Reprinted by permission of the publication.

"Songs of Faith," by Alanna Nash, originally appeared in *Country Weekly* on June 5, 2006. Reprinted by permission of the author.

"Bobby Bare: The Return of the Quiet Outlaw" by Rick Kelly, originally appeared in the April/May issue of *CMA Close-Up*. Reprinted by permission of the author.

"Del McCoury: Leading Man," by Chris Stuart, originally appeared in *Bluegrass Unlimited* in the June 2006 issue. Reprinted by permission of the publication and author.

"Faith Hill Never Stopped Being a Mississippi Girl," by Michael McCall, originally appeared in the Dec.2005/Jan. 2006 issue of *CMA Close-Up*. Reprinted by permission of the author.

"Brad Paisley Moves up from Corn Dogs to Catered Meals," by Peter Cooper, originally appeared *in The Tennessean* on May 21, 2006. Reprinted by permission of *The Tennessean*

"Earl Scruggs: The Godfather of Bluegrass," by Jon Weisberger, originally appeared in The *Nashville Scene* on March 3, 2005. Reprinted by permission of the author.

"Why George Is Still On Top" (George Strait), by David Scarlett, originally appeared in *Country Weekly* on January 13, 2006. Reprinted by permission of the publication.

"Just What the Hell Is Country Music, Anyway?" by Chet Flippo, originally appeared on the CMT.com website in the "Nashville Skyline" column on Oct. 6, 2005. Reprinted by permission of the author.

"Alecia Nugent" by Geoffrey Himes, originally appeared in *Bluegrass Unlimited* in the May 2006 issue. Reprinted by permission of the author and publication.

"Women Make Inroads into Realm of Record Production," by Peter Cooper, originally appeared in *The Tennessean* on May 7, 2006. Reprinted by permission of *The Tennessean*.